TELEVISION REVOLUTION IN RURAL INDIA

About the Authors

Binod C. Agrawal, (PhD-Anthropology, 1970 University of Wisconsin, Madison, USA) is a well-known International Communication Research Expert. He has reputation of being innovative in research methods and techniques, institution building, management and teaching leadership. Founder, Director of several institutions and a University. Earlier he worked for over two decades and pioneered use of qualitative methods for communications research during the world famous Satellite Instructional Television Experiment (SITE), 1975-1976 and lead an inter- disciplinary SITE social research team of over 100 social scientists. Author of two dozen books and several dozen articles in national and International journals and continues to publish.

Munjuluri Venkata Thimma Raju (M.V.T. Raju) born in the East Godavari District of Andhra Pradesh, where he had his early education (M.A. in Anthropology in 1970, and M.A. in Sociology from Andhra University, Ph.D. 1980). Had a distinction of carrying out field research in several collaborative research projects including SITE and published outstanding papers in Anthropology. Raju taught at the Sri Satyasai College, Whitefield and at the University of Hyderabad in 1986 where he proposed the restudy of SITE. Unfortunately, he could not complete the project due to serious illness. A highly promising career came to an abrupt end with the untimely demise of M.V.T. Raju in 1988.

Ponnada Venkata Rao (Ph.D. Anthropology, 1983, Andhra University) Professor of anthropology, University of Hyderabad since 1985. P. Venkata Rao functioned as Head, and as Coordinator, UGC Special Assistance Programme and Dean, School of Social Sciences, University of Hyderabad. Recipient of University Grants Commission's Research Award (1999-2002) and has published five books and over fifty five research papers to his credit. He has also guided fifteen Ph.D. and twenty eight M.Phil. degree students. He has also carried out research projects and consultancies for organizations like UGC, ICSSR, ISRO, USAID etc. and currently editor of internationally known journal *The Eastern Anthropologist*.

Komal H. Shah (Ph.D.—Sociology of Communication, in 2016 from Gujarat University) is an upcoming eminent communication researcher and teacher for over eight years and Digital Communication specialist. Currently Shah is working at Educational Multimedia Research Centre, Gujarat University, Ahmedabad. She is deeply involved in educational television research and educational media production. Shah is recipient of Asian Research Center, Bangkok support to present research papers in the international round table. At her credit there are several publications in national and international journals. Shah has taught both under and post-graduate communication courses and guided Master's dissertation while teaching in well-known media and communication institutes at Ahmedabad.

Television Revolution in Rural India

SITE Re-visited

Binod C. Agrawal
M.V.T. Raju
Ponnada Venkata Rao
Komal Shah

CONCEPT PUBLISHING COMPANY PVT. LTD.
NEW DELHI-110059

ISBN-13: 978-93-86682-95-6

First Published 2019

Published and Printed by

Concept Since 1974

Concept Publishing Company Pvt. Ltd.
A/15-16, Commercial Block, Mohan Garden,
New Delhi-110059 (India)
T : 91 11 25351460, 91 11 25351794
E : publishing@conceptpub.com, *W*: www.conceptpub.com

Cataloging in Publication Data--Courtesy: D.K. Agencies (P) Ltd. <docinfo@dkagencies.com>

Agrawal, Binod C., 1942- author.
Television revolution in rural India : SITE re-visited / Binod C. Agrawal, M.V.T. Raju, Ponnada Venkata Rao, Komal Shah.
pages cm
Study conducted in Kawadapally village of Telangana, India.
Includes bibliographical references and index.
ISBN 9789386682956

1. Television in rural development—India—Kawadapally. 2. Television in education—India—Kawadapally. 3. Telecommunication in education—India—Kawadapally. 4. Direct broadcast satellite television—Social aspects—India—Kawadapally. I. Raju, M. V. T. (Munjuluri Venkata Thimma), author. II. Rao, P. V. (Ponnada Venkata), 1955- author. III. Shah, Komal (Komal H.), author. IV. Title.

LCC HN780.Z9M3 2019 | DDC 302.23095484 23

This book is dedicated to

Late M.V.T. Raju

Preface

This book emerged out of SITE social evaluation comparative research study carried out in seven states. Andhra Pradesh study was one out of the seven originally conducted during 1975-76 by M.V.T. Raju under SITE research team consisting of Binod C. Agrawal, J.K. Doshi and K.K. Verma who carried out the first field work in the village Kawadapally (now part of newly created state of Telangana) from March 3, 1975 to September 30, 1976. Field-work covered the entire period of one year Satellite Instructional Television Experiment (SITE) from August 1, 1975 to July 31, 1976. Due to premature demise of M.V.T. Raju, the research report did not see the light of the day though the main findings of the study was integrated in the book by Agrawal (1978) and the field experiences of M.V.T. Raju were published in an edited book (see Agrawal, 1985). After almost 15 years later, a classmate of Raju, P. Venkata Rao (currently Professor of Anthropology at Hyderabad University) offered to update the research study and incorporate observed socio-cultural changes that might have occurred in the village Kawadapally by carrying out a re-study in 1992 for about three months. Venkata Rao did write re-study report that remained untouched by anyone including me until very recently in spite of best of our efforts. In the meantime, I took early retirement in 1995. So book had to wait for another quarter of a century. The present shape was given by joint efforts of Komal Shah (researcher, Gujarat University) and myself revived the writing of the book so, the book could see the light of the day with a number of valuable insights of changes in the rural life. Observed changes wherever possible have been added in the book.

It should be mentioned that during these years the world of media and communication has changed beyond recognition after the advent of INSAT satellite television in India and elsewhere. Our recent stimulus to write the book came from the increasing realization that changes have occurred though little in the process in human communication. It seems that media and communication by and large, in India, has been rapidly changing though human communication remained an important means of communication in today's WhatsApp era. Observations support the view that information, knowledge and wisdom continues as in the past, and has been passed on orally from one generation to the other especially in rural India as well as to a large extent in the urban India. While oral communication dominates in day to day life written and other means and channels are increasingly penetrating. Various communication changes that have taken place in India due to electronic and digital media introduction remained subservient to oral communication though media impact could be experienced and felt everywhere whether rural or urban, men or women, rich or poor, Hindu or Muslim and literate or illiterate. But, little research has been carried out or serious attention has been paid by anthropologists to study except journalists who have assessed the role and impact of digital media in bringing about social change.

The collective effort in this book is to describe and analyse the possible impact of satellite television over a span of forty years in an Indian village. Hope the reader will get the glimpses of change in rural India.

July 23, 2018 **Binod C. Agrawal**

Acknowledgements

The book has taken almost over forty years since the village study of Satellite in Andhra Pradesh, now in Telengana was carried out by Late Dr. M.V.T. Raju in the village Kawadapally. The authors especially Prof. Ponnada Venkata Rao on my request decided to restudy Kawadapally almost after fifteen years to understand the process of change that had occurred in the village. In the meantime I moved from ISRO and the project remained in dormant state until a year ago. The project was revived with the help of Dr. Venkata Rao and Dr. Komal Shah.

The present volume is joint efforts, primarily of three authors, namely Dr. Binod Agrawal, Prof. Venkata Rao and Dr. Komal Shah. I gratefully acknowledge the efforts made by Venkata Rao and Komal Shah.

The book is dedicated to Late Dr. M.V.T. Raju, the original researcher who conducted the fieldwork in 1975-76. I am also grateful to the Concept Publishing Company Pvt. Ltd., especially Shri Ashok Mittal, who took special pains to publish this book.

List of Tables

Contents

1
Introduction

Oral human communication seems to be the most prevalent and important means of communication in ancient and modern India. In almost all agrarian societies, knowledge and wisdom were passed on orally from one generation to other except among few literates. Oral and face to face exchange and transfer of information formed the major means of sharing experiences, ideas, knowledge, information and wisdom.

Oral communication has its antiquity in ancient *Bharatvarsha,* now known as India. Two ancient treasure books, written and compiled several centuries before Christian era by Bharat-Muni (3rd to 1st BCE) — *Natyashastra* (some time before Christian era, Ghosh 1951) and Chanakya's (371-283 BCE) *Kautilya Arthashastra* (Rangarajan, 1992) bear its testimony. Both books have made several explicit, oblique and implicit; direct, graphic and indirect descriptive communication codes, means and methods within multilingual cultures and composite Indian Civilization for continuity and change. These theatrical and political economic treasures also have prescribed codes of familial, civil and political conduct. In *Sanatana Dharm*a (popularly translated and referred to as Hindu religion) communication was considered essential for leading a social life that would provide peace, prosperity and procreation as offsprings. On the other hand, the entire method of drama and theatre performance was meant to inspire and motivate the audience while offering recreation to achieve ultimate desired goals of life of happiness, peace and prosperity. The theoretical assumptions of communication were based on the collective and cumulative experiences, knowledge and observations of several centuries.

Other factors that influence, modify and shape human communication include human social conditioning, educational learning, and social inheritance. Without further elaboration and philosophical discourse, it would be suffice to say that there have been continuous debates, discourses and experiments to examine and understand theory and process of communication, means and methods, that would help realign, perpetuate sustainable and continuous socio-culture change without breaking or damaging the social order to achieve peace, progress and prosperity within the Indian Civilization. The oral ritual chanting during worship or sacrifice reflects the continuity of oral communication.

In a broader canvas, several Asian Civilizations have followed separate and unique methods and modes of oral, verbal and written communication to preserve and perpetuate multiple patterns and processes of cultural configuration. Over a period, these multiple processes helped evolve; follow and create new techniques of refinement to share views; pass on messages; transfer information and knowledge; preserve and store mythology; religious scriptures and social practices from generation to generation over several millennia. Similarly, prevailing social disorders and conditions in these civilizations forced decay and disappearance of some forms and methods of verbal or oral or even written communications.

In almost all Asian and Mayan civilizations, the dominant mode remained oral, face to face social interaction for exchange and transfer of information, knowledge and wisdom. These ancient methods of communication continued to improvise, evolve and have survived to the present day. They remained most popular, acceptable and prevalent mode of individual, familial and collective exchange of cultural, social and religious information and knowledge.

In multilingual India, various visual, musical and art forms were evolved over several millennia, though Sanskrit and Tamil continued to be a pan Indian language of literary and transmission of sacred knowledge largely as *Shruti* (oral recitation of scared text from memory over and over again spanning some time several centuries without any alteration), *Smriti* (oral social commentary recitations of prescriptive social conduct that should direct and regulate day-to-day individual and collective behaviour in society) and *Shastra* (codification of selected and well tested oral sacred recitations both in oral and written form sometimes spanning over several centuries emerging from the human memory, experience and deliberations) without replacing or displacing the original aim or intent. The oral methods of communication remained an integral part of the civilization of India (Agrawal, 1984).

In this respect oral human communications in India continued to be the most accepted, dominant, and trusted means and methods of exchange of ideas, information, knowledge, views and wisdom in various domains of human experiences and accumulated knowledge as far as possible without altering the aim and intent of communication.

Anthropological Perspective on Oral Communication

Fisher (1973) has reviewed the primitive communication pattern and indicated that there was greater reliance on oral communication in the absence of writing similar to the Indian villages where reliance continues to be largely on face to face and oral, apart from symbolic and non-verbal communication. In last few centuries as a result of British Colonial rule various changes have taken place in rural communication. Further due to the introduction of electronic and digital media of communication, there are perceptible changes in communication behaviour especially after extensive introduction of smart phone across India. But, anthropologists, for a long time have paid little or scanty attention to understand and analyse human communication as to how electronic and digital media had in past and now in present influenced social change.

The cultural anthropologists had been interested in social transaction wherein social relations between persons exchanging words, ideas that effects power relations. Roles, networks, social structures and organizations were abstracted from such social transactions and exchanges in several field based intensive studies. For most anthropologists, the social transactions have been conceived as acts of human communication without paying much attention to its potential role in bringing about change (Belshaw, 1977:41).

The dominant interests of anthropologists and the inadequacy of understanding of digital communication are reflected in anthropological researches on communication, which were earlier confined to linguistic and human communication systems. Some of the earlier studies in India that covered human communication are those of Dube (1955), Majumdar (1958), Damle (1956, 1959), Hein (1959), McCormack (1959), Marriott (1959) and Gumprez (1964) having core focus to understand how religious messages are communicated and internalized. Descriptive analyses of dramas, recitations, *katha* (story telling) and *Ram Leela* were carried out to understand how religious messages were transmitted to individual and society at large.

Hein (1959) and McCormack (1959) studied how religious values were spread through human communications. Majumdar (1958) in a pioneering study described and analysed human communication process involved between different castes in an Indian village. Marriott (1959) observed changes in the traditional human channels of communication due to the influence of radio, newspapers and cinema in rural India.

Among communication scholars, a path breaking study of Andhra Pradesh rural communication was carried out by Lakshmana Rao (1966) in which two villages having different levels of communication exposure with special reference to urban contact and mass media were studied. Lakshmana Rao (1966) found relatively abundant and diverse communication links in the "prosperous" village, whereas the "stagnating" village had sparse communication links. Earlier Dube (1955) had also conducted rural communication study in Andhra Pradesh.

Gaikwad *et al.* (1973) made an attempt to understand the interpersonal (human) communication process and role of rural elite in an Indian village. They identified various gaps existing in the communication process between leaders and their followers which accounted for slow dissemination of information in the village. It was the large landholding farmers who were making a better use of various social circles and mass media as compared to small and medium landholding farmers. The study pointed that even after the introduction of many agriculture development programmes, the socio-economic structure of the village continued to be highly socially stratified without any perceptible change.

Sinha, Kolte and Arya (1976) studied the process of communication in the administrative system of different states in India, both in formal and informal communication systems. The researchers found that communication effectiveness was influenced by a number of situational variables. The study made a number of suggestions and recommendations to tone up the communication process in the administrative system.

Sharma (1987) conducted a study of Jaipur and Tonk districts of rural Rajasthan. Exposures to both human and electronic media were found to be correlated with the socio-economic status that included respondents' education, income and occupation. It was concluded that higher the socio-economic status of the respondent higher was the exposure to electronic media. The study also found that the human communication were still a powerful source of information.

Hartman *et al.* (1988) studied a village each in three states namely Kerala, Andhra Pradesh and West Bengal to understand the role of mass media in village life. The study focused on how information reached the village through various channels and sources and what role human channels, electronic media and government functionaries played in disseminating development information. They found that among the younger generation, those who were better educated and better-off found to be more exposed to electronic media directly. Oral transmission of information still played an important role in the day to day life of the villagers.

After the advent of human communication research, the communication scholars since 1977 have devoted a great deal of time and energy to understand and analyse various facets of human communication that lead to the creation of human communication research as a separate section in International Communication Association (ICA). A large amount of research articles on the various aspects of human communication have been published after the turn of the twenty-first century related to human communication. Same holds true for other English speaking countries and scholars apart from non-English speaking countries like China, Japan, Korea and India apart from Africa and Latin America where a great deal of researches related multilingual communication have been carried without professional recognition.

It should be mentioned that in the last three decades, the emphasis has shifted for study of human communication in wake of communication revolution of digital media and rapid expansion of satellite communication across world including India. In several research reviews Agrawal (2015) pointed out that the human communication research focus has shifted to the study of development communication. Now, that too is slowly dying (Agrawal, 2015) in wake of economic liberalization and media commercialization in several countries. India is no exception in this regard. In India, major landmark in communication research can be found as a part of Satellite Instructional Television Experiment (SITE) social evaluation described (Agrawal, 1981).

Satellite Instructional Television Experiment

India's Satellite Instructional Television Experiment popularly known as SITE is one of the largest experiments on techno-social communication known so far conducted in 1975-76. In this experiment, an attempt was made to provide instantaneous information for national development to those who were otherwise deprived of such information due to technological constraints. With this bold attempt, India became first country to use communication satellite for telecasting development messages directly to remote villages.

SITE was the vision of late Dr. Vikram A. Sarabhai who thought that national development was only possible if the most advanced technology like communication satellites were used to reach remote villages of India. He said, "The process of education is basically related to dissemination/transfer of information. For the rapid and sustained growth of developing countries, the urgent need is to disseminate information to the masses (Sarabhai, 1969:5)". After a preparatory period of over five years, SITE started on August 1975 for a period of one year after the demise of Dr. Sarabhai.

SITE provided distance neutral system of communication with the intention of affecting behavioural changes among the villagers. This system of communication had two specific characteristics: (i) it was directly available at the doorstep of villagers, living in backward and remote parts of the country; and, (ii) television was available to all those who wanted to view it in a community viewing situation as the television sets were installed in public places like schools and *panchayat ghar* (village council).

SITE Social Evaluation

Social Research Group specially created by the SITE team initiated and carried out communication research for the assessment of SITE social impact. Efforts lead the foundation of communication research in all earnest by inter and multidisciplinary research team that included anthropologists among others. The anthropologists took upon themselves to carry out holistic in-depth qualitative study to assess the social impact of SITE. The present study is one of them which were re-studied after a gap of fifteen years in Andhra Pradesh now in Telangana state and supplemented by several observations. Originally re-study was to be conducted by Late Dr. M.V.T. Raju who had carried the first SITE holistic in-depth qualitative study. But due to Dr. Raju's sudden and sad demise, SITE re-study responsibility was shouldered by Dr. P. Venkata Rao who was Dr. Raju's colleague in the Department of Anthropology at Hyderabad University.

Initial social evaluation study of Kawadapally village, Andhra Pradesh (now Telengana) was presented and published (*see* Agrawal, 1978). This book provides an integrated and longitudinal descriptive analysis of the first and second field studies of Kawadapally. Both studies were carried out under the direct supervision and technical direction of Dr. Binod C. Agrawal, Dr. J.K. Doshi and Dr. K.K. Verma who were responsible for the design and planning of the study. It should be clearly understood that Kawadapally was one among nine village studies (for see detail Agrawal, 1985). After almost 25 years Komal Shah joined the team to complete the study for publication.

2
Study Design

Methodological Approach

In-depth holistic study was one of the most important evaluation methods of SITE social research. The emphasis of holistic study was to describe and analyse what a survey or feedback study could not provide. In other words, the holistic study was expected to provide detailed, descriptive and in-depth answers, in qualitative terms, to the questions at micro-level of intentional and unintentional changes brought about by television in Kawadapally village.

Re-study attempted to provide answer and insights to the process of adoption of development messages. Also, the role played by SITE television in accelerating or retarding development process in areas of agriculture, family planning, health and nutrition apart from primary education and teachers' training.

The social and educational impact of television on primary school going children in the age-group of 5-12 years was an integral part of the evaluation along with short duration two multimedia science education training of the school teachers in which STIE telecast formed an important component of training. In addition the impact study, it also evaluated the impact of common national Hindi programmes among non-Hindi viewers of Kawadapally, it being a Telugu speaking village in Andhra Pradesh (now in Telangana).

Conceptual Difficulty of the Study

The word 'whole' has been part of anthropological studies for long time. But, a question arises whether one can study village community as a whole. According to Redfield (1960) a little community which is small isolated, homogeneous and self-sufficient can be studied as a 'whole'. Though, it is difficult to isolate such type of community, the village was considered as a whole at the conceptual level. The villagers always identified their village members as 'ours' and others as 'they' or 'their'. The village is a part of social, economic and political networks but the social structure of the village is a unit by itself and the village has its own communication pattern. Hence, the present study approached the village as a conceptual whole.

In this study, village Kawadapally has been treated as a conceptual whole and is conceived as a microcosm of the broader cultural region. The village which was taken up for study formed a part of a cultural matrix. It is assumed that observations recorded in the village may be similar and resemble those of the events occurring in similar type of villages which together form a cultural matrix. Thus, the village Kawadapally was taken as a unit of study representing the broader cultural region. The selected holistic study village of Kawadapally need not be a revenue or census village. Those households of a habitation which maintain the identity of 'their' habitation or settlement and separate 'their' village from 'other' villages were included for observation. The term *Jati* has been used to avoid the confusion existing with the term 'caste'. *Jati* is understood to be an endogamous group having exchange of bride and groom relations among them and as perceived by the members of that group as opposed to the members of any such other group or *Jati*. The spread of *Jati* is generally confined within the limited geographic area though due to social mobility it is changing.

The term 'household' is used to denote an identifiable group, where largely relatives whose members take food prepared on a single hearth and live under the same roof. Households form family units which could be characterized by size and composition as single parent family, nuclear family, joint family and extended family. A household could have non-relatives also.

For the SITE holistic study, after serious deliberations and discussions it was decided that the anthropologists would follow *emic* categories in description, analysis as well as in report writing. The *emic* category is defined as those cultural categories that are based on the cultural judgements of its inhabitants, conceived and maintained by them in their daily life within the village under observations. Pelto (1970) opined "the units of conceptualization in anthropological theories should be discovered by availing the cognitive processes of the people studied, rather than those imposed from cross-cultural classification of behaviour. While taking up this approach, the real meanings of village cultural categories have been noted down after examining the total behaviour which includes the non-verbal and symbolic communication".

Village Selection

Three factors were kept in mind at the time of village selection for SITE holistic study. These were demographic, social and communication factors. While selecting the village, it was decided that the selected village should have approximately a population of 1250; the village should be a multi-*Jati* having several *Jati* living in the village and if possible, village should be multi-religious. Also the village should not be near an urban centre to have excessive media exposure. Hence, it should be located at a distance ranging from 20 to 30 kilometers from any urban centre.

The village was to be selected from among four SITE districts. Hyderabad district (presently renamed as Ranga Reddy district), Hayathnagar block had highest number of SITE villages. So tentatively, on the basis of Census of India and other secondary data, nine villages were considered for the study. Kawadapally seemed to have fulfilled almost all criteria of selection. Kawadapally was a multi-*Jati* village; distance from nearest urban centre Hyderabad was more than 20 kilometers. In addition, village followed multi-cropping pattern. The cooperative attitude of the villagers helped in making final decision as that was taken into consideration while selecting the village.

Fieldwork

First fieldwork in Kawadapally was carried out by late M.V.T. Raju under direction and supervision of Professors Binod C. Agrawal (SITE holistic study project leader) supported by J.K. Doshi and K.K. Verma. Fieldwork started in March 1975 after intensive training at Ahmedabad and necessary preparation. The field study was terminated in October 1976 by Dr. M.V.T. Raju covering duration of eighteen months.

The Re-study

Dr. P. Venkata Rao carried out three months re-study of Kawadapally in 1992 having original SITE holistic social evaluation objectives with added objective of longitudinal dimension of change after many fold expansion of digital media now referred to as "communication revolution" in very short span of time globally.

In the first fieldwork late M.V.T. Raju used anthropological methods and techniques of fieldwork for an in-depth understanding of rural communication process and to assess the social effects of SITE. First field study provided valuable data that were available from Kawadapally, these acted as impetus to the idea of re-study of Kawadapally after over fifteen years.

The original SITE social evaluation objectives helped to formulate objectives for the re-study. It aimed (a) to have longitudinal understanding of the changes that might have occurred in the village after the completion of SITE on July 31, 1976 and record these changes, if any, due to television that was continued as post-SITE activity in particular and media in general on village life; (b) to study the changes in the processes of human communication after 1976; and (c) to evaluate long term socio-economic and cultural changes that might have taken place in Kawadapally and the surrounding areas.

Limitations of Re-study

In the past, several anthropologists have conducted re-study in their respective fields to study change and have provided interesting insights. Anthropologists like Firth (1959), Epstein (1973), Gough (1989), and Wiser (1971) have re-studied their original villages to record and assess the changes that had occurred after first fieldwork in their respective field areas.

Another kind of village/community re-study was conducted, like the present study, in which another anthropologist had carried out fieldwork in the same location. Such re-study is not free from controversies of interpretations in the past. Re-study of Tepoztlan of Robert Redfield (1930) and village study by Oscar Lewis (1951), study of Samoans by Margaret Mead (1952) and Derek Freeman (1965) are well known examples for this kind of studies. Reasons attributed to the variation in the outcomes could be due to differences in research technique, orientation, conceptualization of the problem and interpretation. Legitimate changes that might have taken place in the re-study after digital media revolution and changes caused by time gap between the first fieldwork seems very important factor in understanding the change between SITE and post-SITE re-study.

Rao was handicap being new and no rapport, familiarity and acceptance in the village like that of Raju. At the same time being a Telugu speaker and native of Andhra Pradesh with full familiarity of the nuances of language and culture of region Rao was able to conduct re-study in Kawadapally though the fieldwork was of much shorter duration (three months) as compared to the original study.

The short duration of fieldwork and the circumstances of entry came in the way of Rao to establish high level of rapport. Raju's entry into the village almost coincided with the entry of the most novel satellite television of those days and Raju was identified as "Television Officer" in the village. Years later, when Rao entered Kawadapally, he lacked familiarity, orientation and insights of SITE that Raju had.

Rao did not have to start afresh in the field as he followed a preset pattern of fieldwork by using the same classification and categories used in the first study (for example the ranking of *Jatis* into highest, high, intermediary, low and Scheduled Castes). At the same time, Rao faced other difficulties as he could not lay his hands on all the relevant material collected in the original study. Also he was not able to identify informants and households that were covered earlier through case-study and in-depth interviews. Due to short duration of fieldwork, Rao could not carry out desirable level of participant observation. Hence, Rao felt that adequate amount of data compared to the original study could not be collected during re-study though collected data was considered adequate for comparison and analysis over a period of time.

First Phase Fieldwork

First phase fieldwork started in the month of March 1975 in Kawadapally. After establishment of rapport in the first month census was taken up during the month of April 1975 using the standard instrument (see Appendix I) used in all SITE holistic study villages. A location map was drawn to show the location of all houses, important places, trees and lanes (see Map 1). From May 1975 data collection was initiated on the social structure, existing channels of communication, political situation and economy of the village. Methods used for data collection included participant observations, discussions and structured interviews.

From July 1975 data was collected on pre-SITE telecast. During SITE period daily viewers' feedback was collected from school children in the morning and adults in the evening on items such as location of television, sitting pattern of viewer's, size of viewers, level of Hindi knowledge, and opinions on teachers training programmes. After the closure of SITE on July 31, 1976 viewers' feelings about absence of SITE telecast were collected. In addition, secondary data were collected from various offices and documents about ongoing development programmes.

Second Phase Fieldwork (Re-Study)

During re-study Rao stayed in the village for about three months in the summer of 1992. He first collected census data using the original census schedule. It was followed by a number of case studies and interviews supplemented by participant observations. Special attention was paid to identify areas of demographic and socio-economic changes including observable salient cultural changes.

In the following chapters, comparative analysis will be presented of socio-economic changes that were observed due to introduction of SITE and then after lapse of fifteen years of SITE. By then individual television ownership increased in the village and almost no one viewed community television.

3

Kawadapally Over a Period of 1975-1991

The choice of Kawadapally village for in-depth study was based on several considerations which will be described in this chapter.

Kawadapally is situated on the Deccan Plateau twenty six kilometers East of Hyderabad on National Highway No. 9, which connects Hyderabad with Vijayawada. For Kawadapally one has to divert from the all-weather road, which branches off from National Highway No. 9 known as Abdullapurmet to reach to the village.

The geographical location of Kawadapally is approximately on 17°-20° N longitude and 78°-40° E longitude. At present, Kawadapally falls under the administrative jurisdiction the Hayathnagar *Mandal* and Hayathnagar police station. Hayathnagar has District Court of newly created Ranga Reddy District. Prior to August 1978, at the time of SITE study Kawadapally was within the jurisdiction of Hyderabad District. Even after the change Abdullapurmet and Balijagudem villages continued to be within the *Gram Panchayat* of Kawadapally. (*See* Map 1)

Kawadapally is surrounded by villages of Addipalli on north, Kanchelaldugem on north-east; a series of hillocks on east, Batesingaram on south-east, Abdullapurmet on south, Amberpeta on south-west, Balijagudem on west and Taramatipeta on north-west. The village Kawadapally is bounded by shrub jungles on east and west and agricultural fields towards south and north. The habitation area cover is situated on approximately 2553 acres or 1032 hectare area. There is a hillock with a famous temple of Lord Shri Rama on the eastern side of the habitation area.

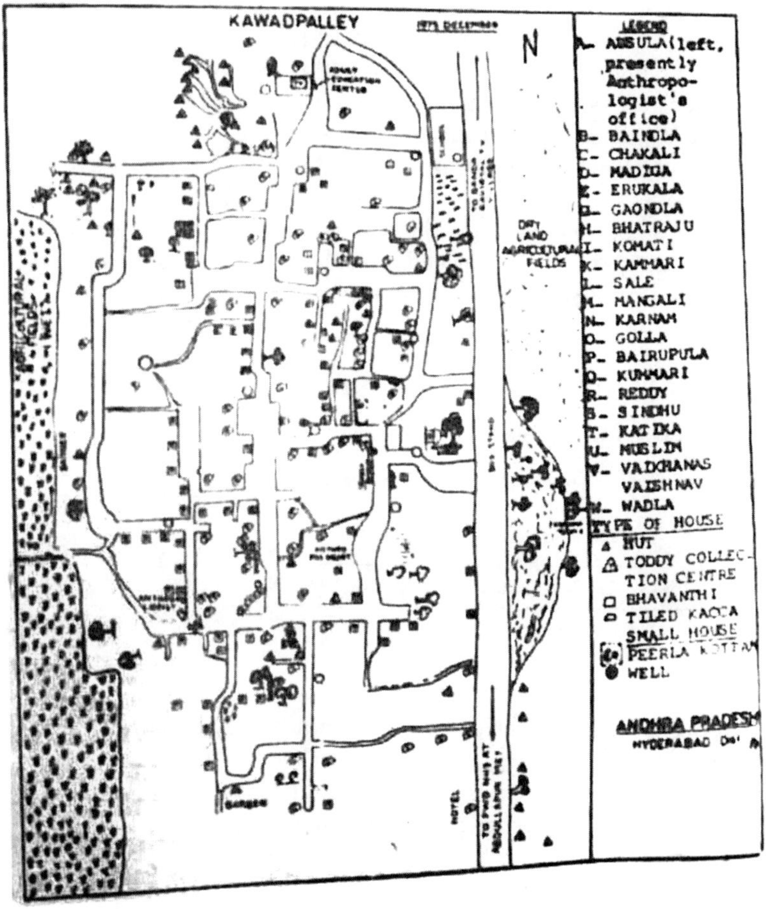

Map 1: *Village map of Kawadapally*

Kawadapally was a medium sized village during the first phase fieldwork. Door to door Census taken in 1975 indicated 221 households having a total population of 1084. According to Census of India 1981 Kawadapally had a population of 1305. The door to door Census undertaken for the re-study in 1991 indicated 220 households consisting of 1324 individuals distributed among the twenty Hindu *Jati* and Muslim. Between the two Census Kawadapally remained a compact settlement. Now in the recent official citations, the village Kawadapally is spelled as Kawadipalle. According to Census of India 2011, the total population of village Kawadapally (Kawadipalle) recorded is 1789 having total households 432. Analysis of data indicated gradual growth of the population of Kawadapally like rest of the rural population in the surrounding villages. Relatively population growth seemed to be higher among Muslim compared to Hindu though Muslim population remained very small compared to Hindu in the village.

Table 3.1: Population Distribution by Religion and Sex

Sl. No.	*Religion*	*Households*		*Males*		*Females*		*Total*	
		1975	1991	1975	1991	1975	1991	1975	1991
1.	Hindu	214	210	513	632	523	639	1036	1271
2.	Muslim	7	10	21	29	27	24	48	53
	Total	**221**	**220**	**534**	**661**	**550**	**663**	**1084**	**1324**

Climate

Three seasons are experienced in Kawadapally. June to October is rainy season (*Vana Kalam*), November to February is winter season (*Chali Kalam*) and March to May in summer (*Enda Kalam*). The first showers of south-west monsoon are expected in the second half of May, which generally intensifies towards end of June and continues till August. North-east monsoon starts from last week of September to first week of November. This period is followed by winter which becomes severe during January and continues up to February. The highest temperature during May is 43°C and lowest during January is 15°C.

Linguistic Zone

The linguistic zone to which Kawadapally belongs is Telangana cultural-linguistic zone where Urdu mixed Telugu is spoken, though largely Telugu is used in day to day personal and social conversation. Kawadapally was under the rule of Nizam till 1948 and prior to India's Independence. After Independence in 1947, it became part of Madras state. Madras state was bifurcated to form Andhra Pradesh and Tamil Nadu. After formation of Andhra Pradesh in 1956, Hyderabad became state capital. After further bifurcation Andhra Pradesh was divided into Andhra Pradesh and Telangana in 2014. Now Hyderabad is the new state capital of Telengana state. Hence, Telugu mixed with Urdu is spoken having mixture of *Dakhini* (Southern) Urdu words. As a result, large scale migration from other linguistic and cultural zones *viz.* Rayalaseema and coastal Andhra Pradesh had taken place in Hyderabad City and the process continues, Hyderabad being major industrial and educational city. The proximity of Kawadapally to Hyderabad City has facilitated continuous contacts with persons coming from across the country and Andhra Pradesh. It has resulted in enrichment of Telugu language and somewhat cultural homogenization and external exposure.

Settlement Pattern

Physical Layout: The habitation of Kawadapally is bound by agricultural fields on three sides *viz.* north, west and south. Lord Shri Rama temple is situated towards the east of the settlement on the hillock. The road connecting the village with Abdullapurmet towards south and Bandar Ravingal towards north separates the hillock from the habitation boundary of Kawadapally. The new extension that took place after 1977 is towards the east of the village. So landmark for entry in the village is Hanuman Shrine connected by a *Kachcha* road just at the base of the hillock. The same *Kachcha* lane divides and separates the village into two identifiable areas by Pedda Bazar ground. There are two more lanes running parallel to Pedda Bazar in the village. These three lanes are connected by several by-lanes.

The shrines of the village goddesses *Eedamma* and *Pochamma* are located amidst the fields towards north-west of the settlement. The other historical landmarks of the village are Boddurai which is situated on south-west corner of the habitation. Fort like structure Kotegodalu is in the ruins located a little away from Boddurai. These two landmarks of the village indicate the location of earlier settlement of the village and its historicity.

Wadloni Dhatti (Central Place)

Wadloni Dhatti is the central place of village having a large open space surrounded by the provision shops and the butchers' houses.

Village Social Layout

The village house layout roughly reflects the social position and social hierarchy and *Jati* composition within the village habitation. The households which belong to the higher socio-economic *Jati* hierarchy occupy either the central or strategic areas of the habitation or on the road side.

The houses belonging to Komati, Gudati, Gaondla and Mustigolla *Jati* who are either economically well off or numerically strong in the village are occupying the central place of the village. The house of the village *Panchayat* president is situated beside the road near the Hanuman Shrine. *Jati*-wise location of houses indicates highest, higher and intermediate *Jati* houses are located in the centre of village. The houses of the lower *Jati* are located in the south area known as *Chakalolla Vadakattu*. The households of Mangali and Chakali *Jati* are also largely located in south area. The households of Madiga, Sindhu and Baindla are located in the north part of the habitation. Period of settlement is also indicated by the location of the house in the village. Late entrants are seen to be occupying away from the central areas of the village. It is said that in the past, there used to be physical separation between residences of different *Jati*, especially in the Madiga (*Harijan*) area. Over a period of time, it was observed that the physical separation between the houses of different *Jati* has begun to disappear due to population explosion and expansion of houses in the village.

Religion and *Jati*

Kawadapally is multi-religious village having both Hindu and Muslim population though Muslim Gaondla form a small percentage in the total village population (Table 3.2). It should be clearly mentioned that dynamics of *Jati* hierarchy and inter-*Jati* interaction and relationships seem to be in flux all the time in the village. Further dynamic phenomenon of *Jati* hierarchy has been changing over a period of time based on economic and political

Table 3.2: Categorization of *Jati,* Their Traditional Occupation, Number of Households

Highest *Jati*	Traditional Occupation	Number of Households	
		1975	1991
Vaikharna Vaishnava	Priest	1	1
Golkonda Vyapari	Cultivation	1	1
Total		**2**	**2**
High *Jati*			
1. Komati	Trade	3	5
2. Gudati Reddi	Agriculture	64	62
3. Mustigolla	Cattle rearing	21	19
4. Katika	Butcher	1	1
5. Kummari	Potter	1	1
6. Bhatraju		2	-
	Total	**92**	**88**
Intermediate *Jati*			
1. Sale	Weaver	4	4
2. Gaondla	Toddy Tapping	65	61
3. Kammari	Smith	3	2
4. Wadla	Carpenter	2	2
5. Ausula	Gold Smith	1	1
6. Muslim	Labour	4	10
	Total	**79**	**80**
Low Jati			
1. Mangali	Barber	3	4
2. Chakali	Washerman	14	14
3. Bairupula	Mendicant Beggar	1	1
4. Erukula	Basket making, swine herding	2	4
	Total	**20**	**23**
Scheduled Castes			
1. Baindla	Labour, cultivation	3	2
2. Madiga	Labour, Cultivation	15	18
3. Sindhu	Folk Performances (Bhagavatham)	6	5
	Total	**24**	**25**

power of a *Jati*. Hence, the present analysis portrays a dynamic analysis as it was observed in 1975 and 1991 over a period of fifteen years. That too, when Hyderabad was changing rapidly due to the internal and external migration of population. So for the analysis of *Jati* hierarchy and their interrelationships, all the *Jatis* of the village have been classified into five recognizable social categories as shown in Table 3.2. The social ranking of *Jati* are suggested and observed by the anthropologists and villagers. According to Table 3.2, Vaikhanansa, Vaishnava and Golkonda Vyapari *Jati* have ranked in the first top social category. It is because the villagers believe that they belong to the Brahmin *varna*. Members of Scheduled Castes like Madiga, Baindla and Sindhu have been grouped in lowest social category. The *Jati* which claim ritually superior status in the village, next to that of the Brahmin, and the villagers accept such a claim are included in social category two. These *Jati* are Komati, Gudati, Mustigolla, Katika, Kummari and Bhatraju. The *Jati* who does not accept food from *Jatis* like Mangali and Chakali (who provide services) but are looked down upon by high *Jati* are included in the intermediate *Jati* category.

Dhatti *Jati* has been kept separately because of their peculiar relationships that include Muslim and Pancha Brahma *Jati*. The social position of Muslim is highly ambiguous and so are attitudes of Hindu towards Muslim in the village. It was observed that Muslim move freely and interact with Madiga and other untouchable *Jati* in their day-to-day life. The high *Jati* allows Muslim into their houses as well as touch them. On occasions like marriage, the Muslims are invited to cook food as they are thought to be expert cooks. In Table 3.3, three *Jatis* of Pancha Brahma are shown separately as they do not exchange brides and grooms amongst themselves. Their position is also somewhat ambiguous in the *Jati* hierarchy as they claim a ritual status equal to that of Brahmin though such a claim is not accepted by the other *Jati*. At the same time, three *Jatis* of Pancha Brahma maintain a distinct identity and do not accept food from other *Jatis*. Hence, they are placed in the intermediate *Jati*.

The service giving *Jati* like Chakali and Mangali along with those of Erukula and Bairupula are considered higher than untouchable, but none of the three categories of highest, high and intermediate *Jatis* consider them as equal. Hence, they are put in the fourth category consisting of low *Jati*.

Further, analysis has been done on the basis of these categories. Table 3.3 gives the population distribution in different *Jati* categories. The other method of defining social *Jati* hierarchy in the village could be defined the way village is inhabited by various occupational Hindu *Jati* who provide *Jati* related services to other Hindu *Jatis* in the village.

Table 3.3: Household Population Distributions by *Jati* and Social Hierarchy

Jati Hierarchy Category	Number of Households		Total Persons		Percentage in the population		Males		Females	
	1975	1991	1975	1991	1975	1991	1975	1991	1975	1991
Highest *Jati*	3	2	8	5	8.0	0.37	5	4	3	1
High *Jati*	92	90	448	536	41.1	40.48	224	272	224	264
Intermediate *Jati*	82	80	421	504	38.7	38.0	213	248	208	256
Low *Jati*	20	23	100	130	9.1	9.8	44	66	56	64
Scheduled *Jati*	24	25	112	149	10.3	11.25	50	71	62	78
Total	**221**	**220**	**1089**	**1324**	**100**	**100**	**536**	**661**	**553**	**663**

Language

Earlier, the language spoken in the region was discussed. In this section, the spoken language in the village will be described and discussed. Observations indicated that language spoken and understood by one and all living in Kawadapally is Telugu. There are ten Muslim households who reported that their mother tongue was Urdu. Among the 210 households whose mother tongue is Telugu 42 heads of the households claimed that they could speak and understand Hindustani also. Of these 17 persons claimed that they could even follow English (also see Table 3.4).

The Urdu speaking persons were also well versed in Telugu and Hindustani (Table 3.4). Those who claimed to be bilingual and especially persons knowing English were more from higher *Jati*. The percentage of those who could speak one or two additional languages apart from Telugu had slightly increased from 1975 to 1991. This could be attributed to growing urban contact and education in the village.

Household Size

The most common household size was 6-9 in Kawadapally

Table 3.4: Percentage Distribution of Households by Languages Spoken by *Jati* Categories

Sl. No.	*Jati Hierarchy Categories*	*Total Households*		*Only Telugu*		*One* Additional*		*Two ** Additional*	
		1975	1991	1975	1991	1975	1991	1975	1991
1.	Highest	3	2	66.7	50.0	33.3	30.0	–	–
2.	High	92	90	73.9	72.2	23.9	18.8	2.2	8.8
3.	Intermediate	82	80	79.3	68.75	19.5	20.0	1.2	11.25
4.	Lower	20	23	90.0	82.60	10.0	17.39	–	–
5.	Scheduled Castes	24	25	100.0	84.0	–	16.0	–	–
	Total	**221**	**220**	**80.0**	**73.18**	**18.6**	**19.9**	**1.4**	**1.72**

* Mostly Hindustani.
** English.

followed closely by households having 2-5 members. Table 3.5 shows the percentage distribution of household sizes in different *Jati* categories. Table 3.5 shows that as compared to 1975, there was an increase in the percentage of households having larger number of members. Households having 2-5 were more in number in 1975, but in 1991 households having 6-9 members were more in number. Single person households were less in 1991 when compared to 1975. These changes may be due to the phases of the developmental cycle of the households or changing economic condition of the households.

Table 3.5: Percentage Distribution of Household Size by *Jati* Categories

Household Size	*Highest Jati*		*High Jati*		*Intermediate Jati*		*Lower Jati*		*Scheduled Castes Jati*		*Average*	
	1975	1991	1975	1991	1975	1991	1975	1991	1975	1991	1975	1991
Single Member	33.4	50	10.9	2.22	3.7	2.5	5	–	–	–	6.8	2.2
2 to 5	66.6	50	51	43	51.3	41.21	50	52	66.7	44	52.9	3.6
6 to 9	–	–	34.8	45.5	42.6	45	45	43.4	33.3	44	38	4.5
10 to 13	–	–	2.2	6.6	2.4	7.5	–	–	–	12	1.8	6.8
14 and above	–	–	1.1	2.22	–	3.7	–	4.3	–	–	5.0	2.7
Total Households	**3**	**2**	**92**	**90**	**82**	**80**	**20**	**23**	**24**	**25**	**221**	**220**

Primary Occupation

Out of 220 households in Kawadapally in 1991, toddy tapping and labour work formed the main source of livelihood for ninety households. For another fifty nine households cultivation remained a major source of livelihood. Other occupations pursued by the villagers included business (15), employment (25), *Jati* related occupation (29) and others (2) (Table 3.6). A comparison with 1975 figures reveal a decline in the number of cultivators and a corresponding increase in the number of households depending on labour work. Employment also was on the increase while *Jati* related occupations were on the decline. These changes reflect ongoing socio-economic changes in the village. While there was an overall decline in cultivation as the major occupation, this decline was more pronounced among intermediate *Jati* and Scheduled Castes *Jati*. Correspondingly, the number of labour households among Scheduled Castes *Jati* has increased. Increasing dependency on employment could be observed among high *Jati* and Scheduled Castes *Jati*. *Jati* related occupations were on the decline among intermediate *Jati* and Scheduled Castes *Jati*, whereas among higher *Jati*, *Jati* related occupations had increased.

Table 3.6: Percentage of Households by Household Primary Occupation and *Jati* Categories 1975-1991

Occupation	*Number of Households*		*Highest Jati*		*High Jati*		*Intermediate Jati*		*Lower Jati*		*Scheduled Castes Jati*	
	1975	1991	1975	1991	1975	1991	1975	1991	1975	1991	1975	1991
Cultivation	92	59	2.2	–	71.7	98.3	14.1	–	–	–	12	7
Labour (including toddy tapping)	59	90	–	–	10.2	12.2	83.1	63.5	1.7	2.2	5.1	20
Business	14	15	–	–	71.4	46.6	21.4	53.4	7.1	–	–	–
Employment	16	25	6.3	–	25	40	43.8	28	18.8	20	0	–
Jati related occupations	32	29	–	6.8	3.1	13.7	25	13.7	43.8	55.1	28.1	10.3
Income from other sources	8	2	–	–	62.5	-	25	100	12.5	–	–	–
Total	**221**	**220**	**3**	**2**	**92**	**90**	**82**	**80**	**20**	**23**	**24**	**25**

Agriculture

Agriculture continued to be an important occupation in Kawadapally for majority of households. Since irrigated land was limited and dry crops enjoy prime source of income in the village economy as indicated in Table 3.7. Out of the 220 households, 59 depended on cultivation as the primary occupation. Apart from these owner cultivators, others like cultivator-labourers, share croppers and tenants also depend on cultivation.

Non-cultivating landowning households lease their land to tenants or act as share croppers. Small landowing cultivators for survival also opt for labour work and often accepted share cropping or became land tenants to supplement their merge income. Between 1975 and 1991, the increase in the number of landless can be seen from Table 3.8. A decline in the number of large land-holdings and a corresponding increase in the small, marginal and medium sized landholdings can also be observed due to family property division. It was no accident that 23 households of lower *Jati* still follow their *Jati* related occupation instead cultivation as their primary occupation both in 1975 and in 1991. This can also be because of their involvement in *Jati* related occupations like hair cutting and washing which remained specialized and primary source of income. Even in the intermediate *Jati* agriculture as the primary occupation had declined between 1975 and 1991.

Table 3.7: Profile of Village Land

Total Area	*1031.5 (in Hectares)*
Forest Area	467.01
Cultivable Waste	141.64
Area not available for cultivation	96.72
Un-irrigated Land	273.16
Irrigated Land	35.21
Land Irrigated by Tank	18.62
Land Irrigated Under Wells	4.45
Land Irrigated by Wells (with electrical pump sets	12.14

Source: Mandal Office, Hayathnagar.

Crops, Cropping Pattern and Fertilizer Use

In Kawadapally, major food crops are *Jowar* and *Bajra* followed by

Table 3.8: Percentage Distribution of Households by Landholding in Hectare and *Jati* Categories 1975-1991

Lan holding	Total Households		Highest Jati		High Jati		Intermediate Jati		Lower Jati		Scheduled Castes Jati	
	1975	1991	1975	1991	1975	1991	1975	1991	1975	1991	1975	1991
Landless	85	109	–	100	20.7	22	56.1	58	45	17	45.8	10
Marginal 1 & less than 1	11	25	–	–	1.1	7	2.4	4	20	6	16.7	8
Small 2 to 3	18	31	–	–	1.1	15	18.6	9	25	–	16.7	7
Medium small 4 to-5	9	21	–	–	7.6	14	6.1	7	10	–	20.8	–
Medium 5 to 10	34	22	–	–	25	20	13.4	2	–	–	–	–
Large 11 to 20	27	4	66.7	–	21.7	4	4.9	–	–	–	–	–
Very Large 20+	24	8	33.3	–	22.8	8	2.4	–	–	–	–	–
Total	**208***	**220**	**3**	**2**	**92**	**90**	**82**	**80**	**20**	**23**	**24**	**25**

* In the preparation of this table only 208 households have been considered for analysis in 1975 and 220 in 1991, hence there is a minor variation in the total number of households in 1975 census.

Paddy, Ginger, Chillies, Tobacco and Vegetables like Sour Gourd, Tomato, Brinjal, Lady Fingers and country Beans. They are cultivated on small patches of land. Castor and groundnut form two important commercial crops. Horse gram, Red gram and Green gram are cultivated as mixed crops with *Jowar* and *Bajra*.

Food Crops: The cash crops include Paddy, *Jowar* and *Bajra*. Of these Paddy is cultivated in land irrigated by wells and tanks. In general, three crops are grown in a cropping year for cultivating Paddy. But those who depend on tank irrigation grow only one Paddy crop. The first crop season locally known as *Chintapuvva Karthi* starts in mid-May and ends by late August. The second crop season is *Vanakalam Panta* which starts in September and ends in January. The third crop season starts in late January or early February and ends by late April. In the first and third cropping seasons short duration crops are grown.

Fertilizer and Seed Use: Chemical fertilizers are being used that started in early seventies of last century onwards. So, are hybrid varieties seed like *Hamsa*, *Jaya*, I.R.B., and *Jagannath*. These were grown as short duration crop for the first time in 1974-75. Conventional seeds continued to be used for long duration crops like *Vanakalam Panta*.

Bajra and *Jowar* are grown in rain fed land. Natural manure from cattle and goat dropping is used for these crops. Chemical fertilizer is not used on dry land. Groundnut is sown when there is sufficient rain. For groundnut only natural manure is used. Castor is one crop for which multiple turning over of the field has to be done several times. Same is repeated during harvesting of castor. Now hybrid varieties of castor seeds are being used for castor cultivation.

Cash Crops: Vegetables as cash crop are cultivated in small patches of land adjacent to the paddy fields. Table 3.9 shows the cropping pattern in Kawadapally during 1990-1991.

As seen in Table 3.9, chemical fertilizers and high yielding varieties of seeds are used only for paddy and castor crops which are grown in lands irrigated by wells.

Table 3.9: Cropping Pattern in Kawadapally in 1990-1991

Crop	*Wet Land (in hectares)*	*Dry Land (in hectares)*	*Source of Irrigation*	*High Yielding Varieties/Ordinary Seeds*
Paddy	20.0	–	Wells, tanks	High Yielding Varieties
Jowar	–	82	Rain fed	Ordinary
Bajra	–	28	Rain fed	Ordinary
Green gram	–	2	Rain fed	Ordinary
Red gram	–	12	Rain fed	Ordinary
Vegetables	12	–	Wells	Ordinary
Groundnut	–	1	Rain fed	Ordinary
Sesame	–	2	Rain fed	–
Castor	–	105	Well	Ordinary/Hybrid
Fodder Crops	–	3	Rain fed	–

Source: Mandal Office, Hayatnagar.

Toddy Tapping: Toddy tapping is the second major occupation of the Kawadapally households. The Gaondla *Jati* whose traditional occupation is toddy tapping constitutes the highest number of households (65). For majority of them toddy tapping is the primary occupation. Toddy tapping is a complex economic activity. The major season of toddy in Kawadapally is from January to March. This season is known as *Perupu* (tender) palm season. By the first week of March each palm tree needs three climb ups, first during early morning, second during forenoon and third in the evening for collecting toddy. The evening toddy is known as *Maapati Kallu.* It was observed that by and large *Maapati Kallu* is liked most. The peak season starts from the middle of March and continues till the beginning of May. May is a very hot month and *Parupu* palms are termed as *Karralu* and the yield drops as compared to March-April. From the end of May or first week of June, the season for *Pandu* (fruit) palm starts and reaches its peak by the last week of June. By the end of July, the yield slowly tapers off. August through October is a slack season for toddy tappers. Selling of toddy is carried out either in bean bottles by toddy tappers or individuals visit toddy tappers' households at convenient time and drink there itself. The mode of payment is annual, monthly and spot payments.

Changes in Toddy Business

During 1975, all the toddy trees were in the hands of contractors who used to lease them through auction. Gaondla toddy tappers in turn would sub-contract the toddy trees from the contractors by giving a guarantee that they would provide a stipulated quantity of toddy. The contractors also used to employ some of the Gaondla to work as wage earners. The contractors used to employ *Muneems* (accountants) whose role was to supervise the collection of toddy from Gaondla workers and the sub-contractors.

By 1991, the State Government enacted a new policy in favour of toddy tappers to eliminate middlemen contractors, so, that the toddy trees could be directly leased/transferred to Gaondla toddy tappers. As a result of this change all the toddy trees in the village have become the property of the Toddy Tappers Cooperative Society. Now, the Society distributes toddy trees among its members for toddy tapping. Members pay to State government Rs. 15 per tree through the Cooperative. With this change toddy is collected from the Cooperative Society by the contractors who have become toddy collectors. They are responsible to transport it to the city and are also responsible to pay excise duty.

No excise duty is levied by government for the toddy which is consumed in the village. Hence, toddy has become cheaper in the village than in the market-place or in the city shops. Those who travel through Kawadapally can consume toddy by taking advantage of low price. At many Gaondla houses, toddy is available from morning to night along with various kinds of eatables. Now, for Gaondla toddy is lucrative business. As a result, Gaondla houses in the village look well-kept, new and better when compared to other houses including Gudati *Jati* houses. The removal of the middlemen and the creation of cooperative have helped Gaondla to achieve economic prosperity.

Decline of Barter Exchange

Among Scheduled Castes *Jati* like *Madiga* who have had barter exchange of annual labour in return of grain are known as *Madigatanam.* According to this pattern of exchange each *Madiga Jati* household has had a long standing of understanding with a set of cultivator households, which are to be provided with labour during soil preparation, transplantation, and weeding, harvesting, threshing and transporting grain from field to the market or mill. In return, *Madiga* households received predetermined amount of grain from the cultivator. *Madigatanam* method which had seen declining trend after 1975 almost saw its disappearance under the pressure of market economy by 1991. During re-study it was observed that *Madiga* worked on an annual contractual basis that too only on cash payment instead of kind of agricultural product and has replaced *Madigatanam* as an age old understanding involving cash as preferred mode of payment and sometimes in kind.

Dress Pattern

The most common garment for male adults is *dhoti* and *sari* for women. The young men have now taken to *lungi* when they move in the village. Wearing of *lungi* is said to have started in the sixties and has replaced *dhotis* since then. In 1991, young men were seen wearing trousers especially when they went out of the village. On occasions like marriage, the in-laws present pants and shirts stitched in the village. Men wear *angi* (shirt) as upper garment while females wear *ravika* (blouse). The older women tie their blouse at the front whereas the rest have buttons stitched, and some even wear brassiere. By 1991, it was observed that movies and television together have considerably influenced the dress code in the village. Latest fashions can be seen in the case of school and college going youth. *Salwar-kameez* (Punjabi dress) and various kinds of skirts are popular with girls. Parents who were not bothered much about undergarments of small children are now using readymade undergarments and other clothes. Among girls, the wearing of skirts is still rare and after puberty they continue to wear traditional dress.

In Kawadapally in less than fifteen years, one visible sign of change is the presence of regular fulltime tailors engaged in the village. Few households also have sewing machines in their home not seen earlier in 1975. In this respect there is a wind of change in dress code in the village.

Food

Normally, meals are taken thrice a day. Morning meal or breakfast consists of *Jowar* and *Bajra roti* while noon meal or lunch and evening meal or dinner consists of rice, vegetables, milk and meat/ chicken or animal products that are also consumed along with chillies. Toddy is consumed in all the households. The Gaondla who supply toddy consume *arrack* (country liquor). It was observed that consumption of intoxicating drinks like a*rrack* is on rise and on the higher side in Kawadapally in last fifteen years.

The main diet of the Kawadapally villagers varies from season to season. The staple diet during the period of October to March-April consists of *Jowar* and *Bajra* along with rice. Then the *Bajra* and *Jowar* component get reduced and is substituted by rice from July onwards as staple diet.

Material Culture

Kawadapally village continues to have limited furniture and cooking utensils. By and large households have limited kitchen equipment that consists of earthen ware, brass and stainless steel ware. Wooden chairs and cots are common. Changes in the kitchen ware since 1975 have been observed especially among the Gudatis, who were in a better position as compared to Gaondla in 1991. The Gaondla households are conspicuous for the presence of new houses, furniture, vehicles to mention a few. Modern gadgets like watches, radios, cycles, sewing machines, tape recorders, television sets are seen more amongst them. These things have become part of the village life. Apart from Gudati and Gaondla, the houses of traders, employees of R.T.C. (Road Transport Corporation) and schools are also adorned and display several new material possessions.

Fairs and Festivals

Kawadapally celebrates both Hindu and Muslim festivals in large numbers. Table 3.10 indicates the name of six important festivals, their importance, dates and name of the Telugu/Urdu month in which they are observed and the equivalent month according to the Gregorian calendar.

These six festivals are important for the village that allows intense interpersonal and social interaction. These festivals bring relatives from near and far together and help renew the relationships between various caste groups. These festivals induce activities for the villagers to take up various roles in economic, political and social spheres in an otherwise relatively static and routine village life. Festivals also bring a lot of collective activities and social interaction within the village.

In Kawadapally, the famous temple of Sri Rama on the hillock provides an excellent opportunity and occasion to host a big fair during *Sri Rama Navami* (birthday of Sri Rama). This fair attracts visitors from surrounding villages living within a radius of about 15 kilometers.

Table 3.10: Fairs and Festivals of Kawadapally

Name of the Fair and Festival	*Importance*	*Month in Telugu/Urdu Calendar*	*Approximate month in Gregorian Calendar*
Ugadi	Telugu New Year Day	Chaitram	March/April
Sri Rama Navami	Birth day of Lord Sri Rama	Chaitram	March/April
Bonala Panduga	Offerings to the Village Goddess	Shravana	July/August
Dasserah	Victory Day of Sri Rama and Arjuna	Aswiyuja	September/October
Peerla Panduga	Commemoration of the Grand Son of Prophet Mohmed (Moharram)	Moharram	January/February
Kamnui Panduga Holi	Change of Season Burning of Lust	Magha	February

Leadership

Leadership in the village can be divided into two categories: (1) Formal leadership and (2) Informal leadership. Formal leaders are those who have a formal elected /appointed office or a position in the power structure of the village. Informal leaders are those who by virtue of hereditary position enjoy and hold a leadership position and/or have been recognized for their special skill, knowledge, intelligence, wisdom and experience and play leadership role in the village affairs. Informal leaders often also assert as leaders on several occasions. The democratic governance and elective political set up has opened up several opportunities and chance for informal leaders to become formal leaders. Among both these leaders, there are a set of leaders who in the village possess certain special knowledge or skill in passing the relevant and useful information to information seekers. They are often recognized/designated and identified as "communication leaders". Their services are required as and when a difficult or serious situation arises within the village. The villagers approach these informal leaders to seek "subject specific information/advice" who are considered as specialist in the areas of their 'knowledge' and 'wisdom'.

During 1975 study, six formal leaders were identified, and each of them was holding a position in the power structure of the village. Three of them held administrative positions viz. *Police Patel* (village Police in charge), *Mali Patel* and *Patwari* (land revenue record keeper). The three others were elected leaders like the *Sarpanch* (President of the statutory village *panchayat*), the secretary of the Cooperative Credit Society and all the elected members of the *Panchayat* council. Except *Patwari*, all of them were from Gudati *Jati* and all of them who owned land of medium to large sized in and around the village. On different occasions, they acted as informal as well as communication leaders. These leaders, it was observed had certain sets of visitors and acquaintances who regularly sought advice from them. By virtue of the formal position and authority on various administrative matters and in the village affairs they gave advice. The visitors preferred elderly formal leaders as they were considered to have more experience. On such occasions, small groups of visitors were also found to be listening to them attentively. These consultations are generally held in the leaders' houses in the morning hours. These formal leaders, because of their involvement in various political and social activities; enterprises and wide contacts, asserted influence. Villagers seek these leaders' advice on household matters, developmental activities, concerning loan, agricultural inputs and personal family matters. Even after the abolition of the hereditary positions of *Patels* and *Patwaris* by the State Government, the importance of these leaders has not reduced. There are a few informal leaders who come from the households of traditional *Jati* headman or because they are educated, whose number are about ten. They take part actively in discussions held on various issues at various gatherings which could be referred as village 'communication centres'. These informal leaders are from Gaondla (three), Gudati and Madiga (one each) and remaining from Sale and Katika *Jati*. Each of them takes active role in village politics and group formation. Apart from these informal leaders, there are other communication leaders ranging from one to four in each *Jati*. They provide various kinds of information and share their experiences with the villagers. These communication leaders are consulted for specialized information like cattle diseases. Thus, villagers obtain various kinds of information from the communication leaders who may not figure in the leadership structure either formal or informal.

The role of leadership has not changed in the village despite growing awareness and exposure. Persons who are rich because of land, wealth and trade are entrenched in the statutory *panchayat*. Biggest landowners, those having liquor business, lorries, poultry and brick factory are members of the statutory *panchayat*. *Sarpanch* and *Upsarpanch* belong to Gudati, and Reddi *Jati*. Five out of eight members in the *panchayat* belong to Congress (I). While Reddi and Harijan *jati* mostly support Congress (I), the Vyasya and Gaondla support the Bharatiya Janata Party, which is now becoming a force in the village. *Ramajanmabhumi* issue had its effect on this village too which also has a locally important Rama temple. Telugu Desam Party has little support while few Communist sympathizers could be identified.

Amenities

Transport: Today Kawadapally is well connected by a bus service operated by Andhra Pradesh Road Transport Corporation from Hyderabad city. Eight trips ply between 8 A.M. to 8 P.M. Several trucks also ply to Hyderabad carrying toddy and they provide cheap transport service to villagers. Trucks, tractors and tempos are major means to carry vegetables to the city and transport coolies to various work spots. The vehicles owned by the villagers like lorries, tractors, bullock carts, scooters and cycles, speak of the increasing physical mobility in the village. Students, employees and others like traders who commute to the city daily make use of season tickets. Through bus facility Kawadapally is connected to villages like Bajijaguda. By going up to Abdullapurmet, which is three kilometers away one can have access to district buses on the busy National Highway No. 9 connecting Vijayawada and Hyderabad. Bullock carts are used to transport paddy, vegetables and fruits like custard apples.

Education: The primary school which was started during 1961 as a single teacher school was upgraded to upper primary school in 1975. A high school is available in Batasingaram village which is three kms. away. There are two non-formal education centres and one adult education centre in the village. There is also an *Aanganwadi* centre providing health education for children. The village attracted private persons as a potential opportunity and an organization from Hyderabad city has established Venkata Ramana Public School, which operates till 10th class as an English medium school. Students from Kawadapally attend colleges and technical and professional courses in Hyderabad city.

Cooperatives and Bank: There is a cooperative society functioning in Kawadapally since 1963 which finances farmers by providing them short term loans for agricultural inputs. Apart from this, the villagers also make use of cooperatives located in places like Batasingaram, Panchayat Samithi (Mandal) for getting fertilizers, seeds etc., on short term loan basis. Nearest bank available is at Abdullapurmet.

Post Office and Telephone: The postal facilities were started in the village in 1956. The post office is a sub-office under the branch post office of Hayathnagar and covers Kawadapally, Abdullapurmet and Balijaguda. It has facility for dispatch and delivery of registered and unregistered letters and money orders. A public telephone is available in the post office. The nearest telegraph office is at Hayathnagar. It should be mentioned that there was rapid expansion of mobile phones after 1991, now a large number of villagers own and use mobile phones.

Radio, Transistors and Televisions: There were 100 radios (including transistors) and 39 television sets working in the village during 1991. There is nearly a threefold increase in the number of radios available in the village and a significant addition of television sets between 1975 and 1991. Table 3.11 shows the *Jati*-wise position of ownership.

Table 3.11: Distribution of Radio and Television Sets in Different *Jati* Categories

Jati Category	*Number of House-holds*		*Number of Radio Sets*		*Per Household Availability of Radio*		*Number of Television sets*		*Per Household Availability of Television*	
	1975	1991	1975	1991	1975	1991	1975*	1991	1975*	1991
Highest *Jati*	3	2	0	1	0	0.5	–	–	–	–
High *Jati*	92	90	18	45	0.19	0.5	–	22	–	0.24
Intermediate *Jati*	82	80	15	40	0.18	0.5	–	17	–	0.21
Low *Jati*	20	23	1	9	0.05	0.39	–	-	–	–
Scheduled *Jati*	24	25	0	5	0	0.2	–		–	–

* In 1975, the only television set available was the SITE TV.

Newspapers and Magazines: The literate villagers read newspapers when they visit the city. The teachers and other employees buy newspapers and film magazines when they go to the village. The leaders of various associations and caste bodies get relevant literature. The *Sarpanch* receives developmental and publicity material from different governmental agencies. Some persons subscribe to newspapers from Kawadapally also.

There are two medical practitioners in the village practicing Allopath and Ayurvedic medicine. Apart from these, there are three persons who treat ailments. There are two witch doctors locally called *'Mantragadu'* that treat *'Evil eye'* and deal with problem causing spirits. There are several spirit healers in the nearby villages also. One trained mid-wife is present in the village.

There is a primary health centre at Hayathnagar (13 km). In addition, an M.B.B.S. doctor at Abdullapurmet (3 km) is also available for consultation, however majority of villagers do not approach them. In case of emergencies villagers prefer to go to hospitals in Hyderabad city. An auxiliary nurse-*cum*-mid-wife of health sub-centre at Taramatipeta (4 km) looks after malaria, family planning and maternity cases in the area. The primary health centre at Hayathnagar covers the village for immunization, vaccination etc. and undertakes family planning campaign. An *Aanganwadi* centre is present in the village to provide nutritious food to expecting mothers, lactating mothers and small children.

The descriptive analysis presented so far provides a brief analysis of socio-cultural profile, pattern of occupation, agriculture and health situation in the village. The analysis reflects the situation in 1991 with few observations about the contemporary situation in the village. It would not be out of place to mention that several changes have taken place in the village especially in the field of communication not discussed in this chapter.

4

Cultural Communication

Human society is inconceivable without communication which forms its very basis. The capacity of humans to transmit the cumulative experiences, knowledge and wisdom to the succeeding generations formed the basis for the survival and development of human culture and society. The perpetuation of society becomes impossible without established patterns of communication which are oriented towards preservation of cohesion and maintenance of order. In agrarian societies, where oral communication plays a predominant role, communication can be analysed under the categories of interpersonal communication, verbal and group communication. A communication study of the Indian village must include the village social structure; the existing communication pattern and social interaction among households, *Jati and* inter-*Jati* at village level. The following account traces the communication pattern in Kawadapally and the changes taking place under the influence of various factors.

Household Communication

Communication within the household varies with the size of the household. In small households communication is dyadic and oral. Messages related to the household economy, decision making and child rearing find a place in the discussions. In Kawadapally about 43.6 per cent of the households are of these categories that are also referred to as nuclear family. The process of communication can be analyzed by identifying the message source and receiver in the village context. Who makes the decision in the household can be decided by observing the process of communication in the household. It has been observed that the decision making is shared by the husband and wife in the nuclear families. This pattern is different in the households where the family is of extended type.

By and large in Kawadapally patriarchy is most dominant. This pattern is prominent in the extended family where male head of the household tells his brother and son about the work to be carried out and matters relating to the household. The eldest female member tells the younger ones or daughters-in-law about the dishes to be cooked, their quantity and other domestic matters. Mother-in-law decides about the duration of daughter-in-law's visits to her natal home. The head of the household is observed to be keeping some information with him. He instructs brothers and sons about farm work while he himself looks after external affairs. He contacts local knowledgeable persons for clarifications. The other members of the household are informed of the decisions taken on their behalf later on.

In a household of extended family type, the communication process revolves around a few persons. The source generally is the head of the household or his wife. Communication is always face to face. The receivers are the other members of the household to whom the message is delivered by the source. The decision-makers can be identified when the total communication process is complete and feedback is obtained in the way the source desired it.

On the other hand, in household which are small and fall under the category of nuclear family, the decisions regarding the household tends to be shared by husband and wife. For example, the husband tells his wife about the number of labourers employed, crops position and external affairs. He will be telling children what to do and when. His wife tells him about household requirements and activities of children. Here matters related to economy are decided by the husband and decisions on household matters are shared by husband and wife. The message is conveyed directly and the feedback also reaches the source directly.

This pattern of communication in the extended family reflects high degree patriarchy where other members are not involved. Unlike in the nuclear family where decision-making is shared mutually, in an extended family, it is left to senior members. Others consult senior member on various issues and it is the senior male member who in turn contacts a knowledgeable person and provides feedback to other family members. This makes him a channel in the communication process. The junior member directly approaches knowledgeable persons for clarification of doubt only in the absence of head of the household or if they have insufficient information and happen to be at the place where information is being exchanged. In the case of extended family, the head of the household and other senior male members often act as gate keeper, which was observed regularly in the village.

Transfer of power follows patriarchy in which it is handed over from father to son. Unlike in the Gudati *Jati* where communication revolves around agriculture, among Gaondla the information revolves around their own activity, i.e. toddy tapping. But for the content, among Gaondla families also the household communication proceeds on the lines mentioned above. When the head of the household becomes old he leaves the decision-making in the household to the eldest son. The eldest son consults father on the matters relating to marriage, rituals and other domestic matters. The father then becomes a receiver and also acts as a knowledgeable person and decision-maker.

In all the *Jatis,* the situation is more or less same with regard to household communication. When members grow old and become inactive they become passive receivers of information for all decision-making activity though they have a position as communicators of tradition. When head of the household of an extended family passes away, the place will be taken by the next elderly person. This is the stage where the household member may face some problems while receiving messages related to household maintenance. When different individuals try to assert themselves, the communication lines are broken, negative feedback is received. Ultimately, this results in the breaking up of the extended family into smaller units.

Secondary Role of Women as Communicator: In the household, the elderly women become the source of information and also act as a keeper of tradition and initiator of rituals by sharing past experiences with the younger generation of the household. For example in case of *Biyyam Poyedam,* a ceremony where the son's in-law receives rice and certain other items on occasions like marriage, menarche, and death or once in five years to enhance the prosperity of both parents and their son-in-law. For this ceremony, the elderly women become the source and convey messages regarding this traditional practice. For nuptial ceremony also the elderly women of the household become the source of information and convey messages to the boy and girl on how they should behave with each other.

The elderly men attach themselves to their grand-children. They communicate about the advantage of becoming better persons and better behaviour. The elderly teach children about the advantages of going to school, looking neat and tidy. The children inform the mother about the events they come across or hear while they move in the village. They also inform the happenings in the school. In the process of socialization, the child learns several things from the adults in the household. The parents in the nuclear family type of households, male siblings of father in the extended family type; teach the children essential modes of behaviour to respond to various social situations. The elder members of the household are observed to ask their grand-children to say *'Namaste'* to distinguished visitors like teachers, doctors, government officials by keeping their right hand on the forehead. Some of the literate members ask their children to say *'Tata'* to the visitors when they are leaving.

The elder members of the household expect respect and difference from the younger members. Exchange of information in the household reflects this. Those who are not respecting elders or obeying their directives will be commented and criticized by members of the other households.

During 1991 fieldwork, many leaders in the village felt that elderly and aged members are being side lined in the village and also in their own households. With new occupational practices and Non-*Jati* occupations, the experience and wisdom of elders is no longer relevant. Educated younger siblings try to question elders and avoid them. Intra-household communication covers information beyond domestic affairs. Apart from giving an idea of deviant behaviour of various persons, achievements of the members of the other households are also acknowledged. Comparison is made between X getting a job easily while Y fails to get one after prolonged efforts. These kind of exchanges taking place in the household will reinforce expected and approved modes of behaviour.

Inter-Household Communication

Information flows between the households wherever two persons from different households meet. This conversation covers all aspects pertaining to the events which took place in each of the households. Information generated from one household is conveyed to the other households in the neighbourhood and sometimes gets circulated in the village. Purchases made, news related to births, deaths, accidents, quarrels, disputes, agricultural activities and a host of items are passed on in this process. Information at times can be in the form of advices and suggestions also. The information on economic condition or socially unacceptable behaviour of the individual living in another household is also conveyed in the process. Agricultural labourers often exchange information about wages paid to them and also mode of payment and delays. Agricultural labourers also discuss their working conditions and treatment by the landowners. Health information, remedies to various ailments, names of efficient *'Mantragadu'* (magician) also formed part of the inter-household communication. The inter-household communication revolves around occupation related activities and largely centres around agriculture, toddy tapping and labour. The entire verbal communication as a process that starts within the household slowly is passed on to other households and spreads in the entire village. It was observed that there were several places of human congregation which acts as an information centre from where information exchange takes place, which are dynamic and appear and disappear from time to time.

Communication Centres

In Kawadapally, the information is exchanged at several places, but there are some places where villagers meet regularly and talk among themselves what has been referred to as information centre. It should be mentioned that the house of the police *Patel*, the provision shop, the tea stall, arrack shop, tailor shop, drinking water wells, premises of Gaondla where people go in the evening to have toddy, bus stop, milk collection centre are prominent places where many people congregate everyday and in the process exchange information. Of these, the more important places are the houses of police *Patel*, bus stop, drinking water wells, tea stall and provision shops. Other locations where information is exchanged are paddy fields during transplantation and harvesting. Before starting of agricultural season one can observe congregation of the farmers at the ironsmith workshop and carpenter workshop which provide an opportunity for exchange of information and act as a communication centre. Other places where a small group sit to congregate are the toddy collection centres which also serve as communication centre along with places like truck loading locations for toddy which is carried to the city. In 1991, after the change of state laws that permitted selling of toddy from home by Gaondla households, a new set of communication centre has being activated. As the rates of toddy are much cheaper when compared to city, those who are crossing the village especially on two wheelers stop to enjoy toddy. At all these houses *papads* are sold along with drink. One can see vehicles parked outside these houses which also serve toddy to villagers and outsiders. This allows another set of information exchange among the villagers and visitors of other places who often bring new information on variety of related and unrelated topics and subjects. At all these places, the information exchange revolves around individual household, experiences on development and induced changes for betterment of the village.

Patel Communication

Patel level communication can be described under (i) inter-communication and (ii) inter-*Jati* communication. Two types of communication transcend the village. *Jati* communication gets restricted and does not flow into inter-*Jati* level communication if it has some stipulated conflicts. *Jati* level communication takes place when members of *Jati* are present at the communication centre and have information which is of interest for them. But, if any other *Jati* members are present they remain passive receivers of the information, however, such informations are discussed in the respective *Jati* meeting places. It has been observed that wherever information about a particular member comes up, the *Jati* members and villagers discuss various pieces of information, both good and bad, about that particular person. Members of one *Jati* also discuss about other *Jati* and their position.

In the democratic village politics, the assistance provided by the government to the *Harijans* is repeatedly discussed. Cases of adultery are discussed in camera by members of that particular *Jati* concerned if they feel that it brings down the image of *Jati.* For example, members of *Chakali Jati* held a closed door meeting to discuss about the abortion of *Chakali* widow and pressed her to reveal the identity of the person responsible. On knowing the name of the person, they warned him to discontinue their physical relationships. This information was discussed in a hush by other *Jati.* Pamphlets brought by a youth from the city about meeting of the toddy tappers were discussed by Gaondla on one occasion. After discussion, they all went to the city to attend the meeting.

Efforts are made to suppress or restrict information related to a *Jati* and remain confined within the inner circle of the *Jati.* In the other situations, the message coming from outside related to that *Jati* get into circulation among members of that *Jati* quickly when compared with other *Jatis.* Particularly, the message flow pertaining to the development programmes meant for a specific *Jati* gets to that *Jati* and other *Jatis* ignore it. Information about cooperatives meant for specific *Jati* comes under this category.

Communication in Marriage

On the other hand, marriage alliance information first moves within the *Jati* but gets diffused among several other *Jati* members as it involves them also in the final stage of marriage ceremony. Details about eligible boys and girls for marriage are circulated, through visitors of one's own *Jati* living in other villages, since village exogamy is followed in Kawadapally. Each marriage venue acts as communication centre for matchmaking. The marriage takes place at groom's place in the lower *Jati* while it takes place at brides' place in higher *Jati.* The invitation for marriage itself is a communication. Close relatives are invited by sending persons from *Mangali Jati* or *Chakali Jati* in person. In *Kammari, Wadla* and other artisan *Jati,* the invitations are delivered personally.

Death Communication

The message about death is communicated to all relatives by blood or marriage. The occasion brings all the villagers together to express their grief to the members of the bereaved household. Visitors exchange information on several topics when they meet. The cause of death, efficacy of various types of treatment for disease, qualities of the dead person, invariably forms part of the conversation. Various matters related to the *Jati* are also discussed on such occasions. Messages about death are always conveyed by the *Madiga Jati* persons to all the relatives. On such occasions, the discussion at various information centres revolves around death and the family of the deceased.

5

Perspective on Development Communication

The term 'development communication' is an umbrella concept that includes induced change in the village by development agencies like health and family planning, education, agriculture. The aim is to improve the quality of rural life. It is a conscious effort on the part of development agencies that are largely supported or created by the government for improving the quality of life and to increase income and productivity. In case of Kawadapally it being near to Hyderabad city, capital of Telangana (earlier Andhra Pradesh) state, it has a locational advantage in receiving stimulation from the developmental impulses emanating from the urban centre. The ever growing contact between the village and the city, Hyderabad, it has become a significant factor in changing the profile of Kawadapally. While education, employment, mass media and transport services brought the village nearer to the outside world, the activities of various developmental agencies played an important role in ushering new ideas and practices. All these ongoing changes are closely related to the objectives of SITE which are intended towards a progressive transformation of rural inhabitants. Various changes that have taken place in health, agriculture, family planning, education and support provided by the government are discussed in the following account.

Growing Urban Contact

In 1975 itself Kawadapally had substantial population visiting Hyderabad and other urban centres frequently. Employees working in APSRTC, peons in various offices, teacher, police *patel*, mali *patel*, *patwari* used to be frequent and regular visitors to the towns like Hayathnagar, Chowtappal and Hyderabad city. Shopkeepers, traders and the Gaondla who are involved in toddy selling also used to visit urban centres on business trips. Cultivators and vegetable growers made regular trips with different kinds of seasonal produce to places like Mir Alam Mandy (city vegetable market). The *Sarpanch* also used to visit Hyderabad for various purposes. All these urban visitors have been a source of information and news which used to spread in the village in due course. All these individuals were enriching the knowledge of an average villager. The change that occurred in the village life in less than 15 years can be gauged from the number of village employees that rose from 16 to 254 from year 1975 to 1991. Similarly, remarkable changes were observed in the increased physical mobility and transport facilities. At the time of this study in 1991 it was observed that there were cycles (61), scooters (5), mopeds (2), lorries (2), taxi (1), tempos (2), auto trolley (1) and tractors (3). Apart from taxi, other vehicles are used for movement of men and materials. Growth of transport facilities, education and occupational mobility resulted in significant changes in the village. APSRTC buses ply between Kawadapally and Hyderabad city eight times a day transporting large number of commuters. Many of them are availing season ticket facility. Apart from buses and private vehicles, lorries and tractors also help move commuters to Hyderabad.

It was observed that a large number of merchants and traders from Mir Alam Market, Choutappal Sunday Market, Madannapeta Sabji Mandi, Hayathnagar and Koti continue to visit in large numbers. In addition students from Kawadapally go to different educational institutions daily. Also growing interest in cinema adds to the list of regular flow of movie-goers to the city.

Mass Media Contact

The descriptive analysis presented in this section would clearly indicate rapidly changing mass media scenario in Kawadapally as a result of communication revolution that has engulfed Andhra Pradesh and the rest of the country.

Radio: In 1975 itself there were thirty five radio/transistor sets in Kawadapally of which twenty seven were in working condition. The community radio set present at that time was there for about a decade. The enthusiasm towards the community radio set declined after the rise of individually owned radios. During the first fieldwork period of nineteen months (1975-76), five people purchased transistors in Kawadapally. And also during the same period eight sets went out of operation. The operation of the community radio set was not regular in those days as they were located in private houses. The person in whose house the set was located used to play the power charges. To save money, he was not operating the set regularly. The villagers preferred film music from *Vividh Bharati* whereas the *panchayat* radio set has been tuned to receive only Hyderabad station which broadcasts film music for a limited period. Majority of the listeners preferred film music and only three persons claimed that they are listening to agricultural programmes. They were from the Gudati *Jati* and one of them was a teacher. Even among the occasional listeners of agricultural programmes, very few were found to be passing on the information on agriculture and other development programmes to others. They all by and large kept information to themselves. Only in one instance use of information received was observed to be communicated to others. One Gudati youth had utilized the message given by transistor in spraying *Rogor* on the chilly crops. He also revealed that he observed his relatives practicing the method in other village which prompted him to take up the method.

By 1991, the number of radios available in the village had increased considerably. A total number of hundred transistors/ radios were available in the village. Availability of radios per house was minimal among lowest *Jati* and Scheduled Caste *Jati*. Though popularity of film music and other entertainment programmes was continuing, few were following modern methods of cultivation using high yielding varieties and pesticides. The villagers were seen purchasing chemical fertilizers like urea apart from a large number of them using green manure. The villagers were using high yielding varieties for paddy and castor crops especially those having irrigated lands. These cultivators conveyed that they were purchasing fertilizers from the cooperative located at Batasingaram and Abdullapurmet.

Films: During 1975-76 in Kawadapally, 162 households

reported that at least one of the members of their households had watched movie once in a while. Members of Gaondla *Jati* who visited Hyderabad often to collect their payments from the toddy contractors also watched movies. During the months of March to May, the toddy tappers took the tender fruits of palm trees to sell them in Hyderabad. During the period many of them watched movies and returned to village in the night. The milk traders and RTC staff who visited Hyderabad also watched movies. Other commuters also saw movies at frequent intervals. Narrations and discussions on films used to take place at village gossip centres. Some of the advertisements and documentaries were also discussed by the villagers. By 1991, films had become a part of daily life in Kawadapally. The impact of films was such that there was a fan association for a Telugu film star Krishna having its office right on the main road next to the tea stall. With the increase in transport facilities and a number of commuters to the city, the incidence of film viewing has increased considerably. In households where they have cassette record players, film songs are played regularly. For marriages and other village festivals film music through mike sets is an omnipresent affair. Those who do not go to the city also watch many movies on television and video cassette players. The movies, screened on television every weekend by Doordarshan are found to be very popular and now satellite television has multiplied the choice of television viewers in the village. The impact of urban contact and movie watching has resulted in considerable influence on the dressing pattern especially on the younger generation.

Newspapers and Magazines: During1975-76, the village used to get only one newspaper, the teacher used to get a Telugu paper from Abdullapurmet through a Gaondla man. Though in Kawadapally there were no regular subscribers to a daily newspaper. The *Sarpanch* used to get 'Andhra Pradesh', a journal of development information and a religious journal called *Prabha* (published by those following *Bahai* faith). The other households also used to receive *Prabha*, but very few leaders read them. Some members of the Gudati family have been bringing Telugu weekly containing short stories and movie features. The teacher used to act as news reader for the members and gathering of Wadloni *Jati* by reading from the newspapers.

After 15 years in 1991, the number of newspaper readers in

Kawadapally increased substantially. This is due to the increased level of education and individuals who had completed high school and intermediate. All the important *Jati* leaders including the *Sarpanch* and the shopkeepers have subscribed to Telugu newspaper. Various Telugu film magazines are popular with the youngsters. The educated village visitors to the city have made it a habit to bring a Telugu newspaper. Employees get an opportunity to get a glimpse of newspapers at the workplace. One can observe reading of newspaper at tea stall, bus stop and similar public place. Twelve persons in the village have reported that they are subscribing to newspapers. Significantly, seven of them are from the Gudati *Jati* and the other five are from Gaondla *Jati*. Of these twelve, ten members possess television sets and the other two have a radio each. All of them are getting Telugu newspapers weekly. Only one member gets *Bharatiya Janata Party Samachar* and *Jagruti.*

Post Office: The post office started functioning in Kawadapally in February 1956 with the efforts of a member of Gudati *Jati* who later joined as a school teacher. The post office is a branch post office and it received fewer mails prior to 1971-72. After 1972, a party from Survey of India had camped in the vicinity of Kawadapally which led to increased postal use. Between the years 1975 to 1991, the amount of work in the post office increased significantly. The daily average of letters going out had increased from two to fifteen. The significant change observed was due to the villagers who wrote to their employed sons working outside the village and those availing education in the city. Married daughters who were living with their husbands outside the village began to write to their parents. In addition the frequency of sending job applications for employment and application for admission outside Kawadapally had also increased.

The postal items received also increased from an average of five per day to about twenty per day. These included money orders sent by those employed outside, letters from cooperatives, and other credit institutions like banks. The *Sarpanch* (1975) took an insurance agency and persuaded many villagers to take life insurance policies. These villagers get reminders, receipts for premium paid etc. Few individuals get Telugu weekly and newspapers by post. Some of the villagers are also members of various chit funds and they also receive reminders about the date of auction of chit and payments due.

Telephone: After setting up of post office in the village, a public telephone was installed. It was located in the post office. The political leaders and traders especially those who own lorries and transport vehicles are said to be making use of it. Villagers said that it is not much reliable as it remains out of order quiet frequently. After 1991 sudden growth and penetration of mobile phones, the telephone in the post office has limited use.

School: In Kawadapally, school was established as late as 1950s. After several discussions and debates the building site was finalized on the land belonging to the temple. The construction of building was done in 1963. The school which was started as a single teacher school became a two teacher school in 1968. In 1974-75 standard V was added to the school. During 1974-75 attempts were made by the Headmaster to add VI standard to the school. He motivated the villagers to donate substantial amount to the *Panchayat Samiti,* which provided a matching grant equal to the contributions towards the expansion. The school has been developed into a central school in October 1975, which made it a place of weekly meeting of several other teachers coming from six neighbouring villages. The discussions held in the meeting were about teaching, attendance and other problems. These were referred to monthly meetings held at the block office at Hayathnagar. Thus, the position of headmaster as a channel of communication between the teachers of the schools under the central school and the block has been established.

Between 1975 and 1991, education in Kawadapally has increased significantly. The first school started in the village is still continuing as an upper primary school. It has acquired spacious buildings. Children from the village are also studying in the high school at Batasingaram village two kilometers away. An enterprising institution from the Hyderabad city started running an English medium public school in Kawadapally in which quality conscious parents from Kawadapally and neighbouring villages have enrolled their children. At present 53 children are pursuing educations at elementary level and 22 are at high school stage in different schools in Kawadapally. Nine students from the village are studying in various colleges in the city. Four of them are intermediate and others are in degree courses. After 1991, education has taken a quantum jump at all levels.

Apart from imparting education to the pupils in the school,

the teachers also play an important role in communication. During 1975, the Headmaster of the school, who himself owned a farm and was involved in cultivation at his native village, shared inputs he used while rearing of milch animals and poultry rearing. The teacher also carried messages from the external world. One of the teacher played an important role in the communication centre at traders shop. He spoke about crops, policies of government, politics, marketing and political events and happenings at Hyderabad. The teachers coming from different *Jatis* had different interests and the information they brought varied in content.

As early as 1991, the number of students going to colleges and schools outside Kawadapally act as a source of information. Nearly thirty students hold city bus passes at concessional rates and move between the city and the village every day. They bring back information about movies, fashions, political and cultural activities in the city along with a variety of other information. These students are now becoming trend setters for other local students.

Adult Education Centre

An adult education centre functioned in the village during 1975 in the village community hall run by the *Saksharata Bhavan* (Literacy House) of Andhra Mahila Sabha. Its primary aim was to impart education to cultivators above the age of 18 during night time. One matriculate young man from the village was trained and he started teaching. The first day had brought a chaotic situation because many members of the Scheduled Castes *Jati* wanted to enroll themselves as students. The instructor had to close the doors of the community hall in which classes were conducted to avoid the noise. The Scheduled Castes *Jati* members then complained to the *Sarpanch* who in turn called the instructor and inquired him for not accepting them as members. The instructor replied that the strength had been restricted to thirty only and he could not enroll all members. This situation changed in a month as many members stopped coming. To have some members, the instructor started enrolling those who were below eighteen. The centre became dormant during March 1976 as the instructor fell sick but was reactivated after some months.

The activity of adult education is continuing in the village with the adult education centre functioning in the village even in 1991.

Also functioning are three non-formal education centres, aimed at imparting education to drop-outs and those non-enrolled in the age group of 6-14. Two such centres are having students between standard I–IV. The other centre is covering students of standard V to VII. Apart from these units, the Shramik Vidyapeeth of Ranga Reddy district is also conducting awareness classes and training programmes in the village. The *Hyderabad Akhra Jyothi* also organized some cultural programmes during 1991 to motivate people towards literacy. The village is witnessing a host of programmes in the field of literacy. Formal, non-formal and continuing education making the average adult of the village more exposed to various changes. Descriptive analysis of educational situation in the village seemed to be optimistic and positive as more and more individuals at all levels are wanted to get educated though the same cannot be said about women of the village.

Agriculture

Development communication flows into the village in the area of agriculture. It happens to be of two types: (i) villagers of Kawadapally themselves learning new methods of cultivation and bringing it into the village; (ii) Outsiders making them aware of new practices in agriculture. Members of the other villages and officials of government agencies play a major role here.

Information Inflow through Villagers

It has been observed that villagers practicing agriculture, when they visit their counterparts in other villages are invariably discussing their cultivation. In this process they are getting information about new crops, methods followed, inputs and implementations used and yield prospects of crops. As soon as they return home they again talk to others about what they have seen and learnt. Ramulamma had gone once to a village by name Brahmanpally, where she saw people using *Tangedu* leaves (*Ocassia occidentlis*) as green manure and receiving higher yields. Ramulamma, as soon as she returned from Brahamanpally informed the members of the neighbourhood households about the green manure. She called the young man who cultivated her wet land on share-crop basis and told him about the leaves. This innovation was adopted after some days. The *Patwari* then hired a tractor to level his dry land during November 1975. Many cultivators contacted him to know the salient features of the operation. Some villagers contacted the tractor driver and got information on tractor hire charges and economics of having a tractor. Thus, whenever a new innovation was implemented, the villagers grew curious to know about its utility. By 1991, the rich Gudati *Jati* has acquired three tractors which are being put to various uses and also are hired out.

Visitors from Other Villages

The visitors from the other villages disseminate information on the improved methods of agriculture, inputs, and wage structure and crop prospects to the villagers of Kawadapally. This is observed when son-in-laws visit their parents-in-law and daughter-in-laws visiting their parents. When Ramulamma's daughter comes from Bodduppal, she reveals information about the new types of seeds they are using, fertilizers and pesticides. The new inputs and methods are adopted after a discussion and accepted after a trial. One man of the Gudati *Jati* has been trained in compost making in Hayathnagar but finds it difficult to put it into practice because of the care required.

A couple of weeders were acquired in 1968 by the *panchayat* when Japanese type of paddy plantation was introduced. The weeders became useless and rusted. This happened because four to five persons were required for using a weeder. This practice can be adopted by larger households only. On the other hand, use of sprayers, fertilizers and new varieties of seeds continued year after year and the users are increasing day by day. The information about fertilizers has come from Kanchalagudem and a Gaondla cultivator was the first to adopt. The second case of adoption is from a cultivator of Gudati *Jati* who stayed with his relatives for a month in a village where wet lands were cultivated. The fertilizer use has increased in the village because of the subsidies and credit given by the block authorities. The usage of high yielding castor variety started around 1970. This innovation also came in from Kanchalagudem and became popular with increase in castor prices in the year 1974-75.

Flow of Information through Development Personnel

The village development officer's role in development of agriculture during 1974-75 is seen in the form of distribution of hybrid *jowar, bajra,* castor seeds and distribution of application forms for short term loans for fertilizers. During the period of 19 months of fieldwork, the village development officer made a maximum of ten visits. On four occasions, he brought seeds and on rest of the trips he brought fertilizer loan applications. Thus, the role of the village development officer is limited to providing inputs to the agriculturists instead of communicating the improved methods. The literate villagers have been criticizing this kind of ineffective role in not spending time to resolve their questions and doubts.

While purchasing fertilizers and seeds, the villagers have their own preference of shops in Hyderabad. A shop owned by a person from a neighbouring village who was a *Patwari* from Anjapur village is known and preferred for purchase of seeds and fertilizers. The *Patwari* of Kawadapally was also contacting the office of National Seeds Corporation, who introduced *Jaya* and *Hamsa* varieties of paddy in the village. Some of the cultivators after seeing him getting a higher yield tried to purchase paddy from him to be used as seeds. The output and price factor played an important role in adopting high yielding varieties. The Department of Agriculture has put up number of posters and boards at the office of Agricultural Extension Officer at Hayathnagar. Some of the villagers, whenever, they visit the office look at these publicity material.

In 1991, it was observed that many of the cultivators were able to buy fertilizers and seeds, without the assistance of village development officer. Number of visits by the Development officer to the village also reduced and it was said that he would meet only *panchayat* president and other important members. The villagers are now familiar with high yielding varieties and are buying from shops. Though some seeds and fertilizers are supplied through the *Mandal* (formerly known as block) office, they are inadequate. The villagers are now growing a variety of vegetables, which they now take to a nearest weekly market at Choutappal or to Mir Alam Mandy in the city. In the fields around the village one can see vegetables like ladies fingers, brinjals, tomato, chillies and varieties of beans. In vegetable cultivation also the cultivators have acquired knowledge about better varieties through contacts at marketplaces. But in the case of *Bajra, Jowar* and Groundnut, the adoption of new seeds is limited. Among fertilizers Gromor company fertilizers are popular in the village. Urea and fertilizer brand 28:28:0 are also acquired from Farmers Cooperative at Batasingaram and shops at Abdullapurmet a few kilometers away from Kawadapally. As seen in Table 3.9, chemical fertilizers and high yielding varieties are used only for paddy crop and castor. These are grown on lands irrigated by wells.

Apart from these chemical fertilizers, cultivators are using natural manure obtained from cattle. There was no sprayer present in the village during the first study in 1975. In the area of agriculture, those who have wells have acquired electric pump sets and acquired knowledge about their maintenance and repair. After 1991, there were a total number of twenty five electric motor/ oil engines used as pump sets for drawing water from wells and bore wells. Three tractors are owned in the village and are being used for cultivation and transport.

Animal Husbandry and Cattle Care

In 1975, the villagers were already aware of the improved varieties of cattle like hybrid cows, buffaloes and Jersey cows. The villagers acquired information while observing dairy farms in other villages. The police *patel* used to inform the doctor of veterinary hospital, Hayathnagar, whenever there was a cattle disease in the village. The cattle owners normally approached the police *patel* in case of any disease, who in turn wrote to the doctor. The doctor came personally or sent his compounder depending upon the problem. There is also a sub-centre at nearby Anjapur where a veterinary assistant is available. The doctor sends information about preventive measures and inoculations through him. Sometimes, cattle are taken to Hayathnagar for treatment. Highest number of cases reportedly taken for treatment was during July-December 1975. Out of 39 livestocks treated, 15 belonged to members of Gudati *Jati* and 7 to Gaondla. One of the peons attached to the hospital belongs to Kawadapally and he is contacted by many villagers for bringing medicines for their cattle. This young man who happened to be a Muslim became an important communicator along with the compounder. The compounder visited Kawadapally about six times for immunization of cattle during SITE period. Some of the villagers observed poultry farms on national highway while visiting Hyderabad city and evinced keen interest in them. In fact, a person started a farm on a small scale with two dozen chickens, but did not succeed due to loss of chickens. During 1991, it was observed that the Kawadapally farmers were not successful in having poultries. Two abandoned poultries right outside the village stand witness for this. Inability to compete with large poultries and diseases, are reasons given for the closure of the poultries. Otherwise in the area of animal husbandry there is not much change with regards to immunization and treatment of live-stock.

Heath

The vicinity of Hyderabad city held definite advantages to the villagers. The villagers visit various hospitals for treatment and for meeting their ailing relatives. The villagers hold beliefs in black magic, witchcraft (*Mantralu Cheyyadam*) which still continues to hold its grip on the old people. Younger generation prefer allopathic medicines. But villagers visit city hospitals only after local practitioners fail to cure them. During 1974-75, one old man from Gaondla *Jati* and one woman from *Mustgoli Jati* availed the services of Sarojini Devi Eye Hospital at Hyderabad. Similarly, there are others who went to Osmania Hospital, Fever Hospital, Cancer Hospital and other private nursing homes. The Scheduled Castes *Jati* members have been using primary health centre at Hayathnagar. Two Gaondla women also visited PHC to seek advice about pregnancy. The women are also visiting family planning hospital and government maternity home and also Koti Dawakhana (Hospital) if they experienced difficulties in deliveries. One medical practitioner coming from Batasingaram is also treating patients and in complicated cases referred them to city hospitals. A number of people visiting these city hospitals enhanced the knowledge of villagers about diseases, treatment, and hospitals.

By 1991, one registered medical practitioner and an Ayurvedic doctor were practicing in the village. Also there was one woman in the village as a trained mid-wife. Hence pregnant women did not go outside the village for normal deliveries as the mid-wife conducted deliveries in the village. Hayathnagar continued to be the nearest place where a government doctor is available and it has been observed that mostly the lower *Jati* are using the services of Hayathnagar dispensary. The upper *Jati* are availing services of the local practitioners. Also a doctor with M.B.B.S. qualification is available at Abdullapurmet, where the nearest medical shop is available. Few members are going up to Dilshuk Nagar which is an extension of the city. Health worker from Hayathnagar PHC also visits Kawadapally occasionally and offers medicines for small ailments apart from giving suggestions. There is growing awareness among the villagers about the causes of various diseases. Villagers frequently mentioned that irregular food habits, mosquitoes, contaminated water, excessive drinking of *arrack* (liquor), presence of garbage as the reasons for ill health. The *Aanganwadi* also helped to raise awareness about nutrition, immunization and childcare.

Other Government Agencies

During 1974-75, the National Institute of Nutrition has been conducting a project on enhancing the nutritional value of food using locally available material. The target group being expectant mothers and lactating mothers. This project was being looked after by an auxiliary nurse-*cum*-mid-wife (ANM) locally termed as *sister amma* stationed at Batasingaram village. She was visiting Kawadapally on Wednesdays and was distributing vitamins, minerals and medicines. She was also instructing expectant mothers and lactating mothers about the care to be taken in the food intake. The doctors from National Institute of Nutrition, Hyderabad also used to visit the village once in two months and distributed iron and folic acid tablets to school children.

CARE organization has been preparing soybean oil and nutritive maize flour which are cooked and distributed to the school children. It has been observed that the quantity is not sufficient with the increase of enrolment in the school. Kawadapally was also covered by government auxiliary nurse-*cum*-mid-wife who used to visit once in a month to record malaria cases. She was also entrusted with job of supervising slogan writing on the walls about small pox eradiation. But Kawadapally villagers hardly utilized the services of the ANM.

During the 19 month fieldwork in 1974-75 Kawadapally was visited by a vaccinator three times. The vaccinator requested some of the youngsters to get vaccinated to remove fear from the minds of the villagers. Some of the youth obliged him and also helped him in going from house to house. Inoculations are not readily accepted for fear of fever. The *Patwari* was reporting to health centre whenever epidemics were breaking out. This had resulted in PHC team visiting for inoculation and disinfecting the drinking water wells. This was also being done during *Sri Ramanavami Jatra*. All the villagers were aware of family planning programme. Eight cases of vasectomy and ten cases of tubectomy were recorded amongst the villagers in 1974-75. Vasectomies were fewer in number as men preferred their women to be operated upon. This is because of the fear among men that their sexual activity will come down. Another reason given was that the family prestige can be saved even if the women are involved in adultery.

The family planning propagator visited Kawadapally once during 1974-75 fieldwork. They have been enlisting eligible couples for operation and possible cases for future. They also told some of the local women that if they bring a case, Rs. 50 would be given for motivation. It was observed that family planning awareness was relatively well disseminated in Kawadapally. But, the villagers were indifferent for fear of losing sexual vitality and other after effects. Some wanted assurance that vasectomy could be reversed in case they lose their offspring by accident. A few who were afraid said they would be willing if follow-up action was provided. The villagers were aware of indigenous methods of abortion, which were used whenever unwanted conception took place. Knowledge of pills and other contraceptives was also known based on the recommendation of some doctors.

One local provision shop carried Nirodh in its stock but the shopkeeper reported no sales except children using them as balloons. Here, it is significant to note that between 1975 and 1991 the total population rose from 1069 to 1324, but the number of households remained the same. There was slight increase of population among low *Jati* and Scheduled Castes *Jati* while a small reduction was observed among higher, high and intermediate *Jati*. Since the number of households remained almost the same, the growth in the population reflected an increase of household sizes having 6-9, 10-13, 14 and above members. On the other hand, the percentage of single member household and 2-5 members household showed reduction.

Development Programmes

The landless labourers in the village received *pattas* (certificates) from the government in which land to the extent of about 1.5 acres was allotted during 1966-70. Government also sanctioned house sites to the members of other than Gudati *Jati* in 1975. These lands were distributed from government waste land. The cooperative institutions were utilized for mortgaging land by several villagers. The villagers who received land from government were very enthusiastic on availing loans. During 1974-75, thirty six cultivators had taken long term loans from the land mortgage bank, Hyderabad either for digging wells or for buying pump sets. About 20 of them were successful in utilizing the loan. Others either misused the loan or failed under various circumstances. Thirty members of the village formed into a multi-purpose cooperative and have taken short term loans. Half of them were Gaondla *Jati* young men who utilized the loan for toddy business. About 34 members also joined a cooperative society at Batasingaram motivated by the Gaondla young man. They made efforts and got loans. All these experiences and the State Government's policy of eliminating middle men have led to the formation of a cooperative for toddy tappers which had been functioning effectively by 1991.

As indicated earlier, the toddy tappers cooperative replaced the system of private contractor participating in the auction of toddy-trees and controlling the toddy collection business. The toddy tappers cooperative takes care of the interests of the Gaondla *Jati*. In spite of these efforts, the toddy contractors responsible for transport of toddy continued to sell to the outlets in the city. During 1974-75, efforts were made to acquire pump set and electric power connection for a community well. The community well was located in the Scheduled Castes neighbourhood. Things moved only after some efforts that were made through the BDO, Hayathnagar, as the junior engineer showed reluctance to cooperate. By 1991, electric pump set became functional and water was provided in Kawadapally through the public taps. The *gram panchayat* also acquired two additional buildings through the funds obtained from Jawahar Rojgar Yojana. The *panchayat* also was maintaining electric street lights and other amenities. The villagers often discussed the *panchayat* affairs especially the utilization of funds.

Wind of Socio-Cultural Change

Kawadapally village has been witnessing several changes over a period of years. Various development agencies played a role in transforming agricultural activity, presence of wells and electrified pump sets facilitated in this transformation. Changes could be seen in education and health. Apart from the government agencies, the urban contact and urban opportunities played a significant role in ushering changes in various spheres. One could see visible signs of horticulture expansion all-around the village in response to the market available for vegetables in city. The urban expansion was at the doorsteps of Kawadapally in the form of housing sites and plots being advertised for sale in Hyderabad newspapers at Abdullapurmet and Batasingaram which was less than three kilometers distance from Kawadapally.

6

Arrival of Television in Kawadapally

A television set of 20 inches black and white was installed as a part of the Satellite Instructional Television Experiment (SITE) which started functioning on August 1975. The set was operational till July 1976 and facilitated community viewing. After a gap of nearly ten years television re-entered the village life. Villagers started buying their own television sets to watch Doordarshan programmes telecast from Hyderabad Kendra. The following account gives a detailed assessment of the SITE television in Kawadapally which is followed by an appraisal of the Television in 1991.

The initial village selection team of Satellite Instructional Television Experiment (SITE) visited Kawadapally on April 19, 1974. The team visited the school and community hall, and preferred to put up the television at the community hall. Presence of electrical power connection and a *pucca* building led to the selection of community hall though it was in one corner of the village. The deployment team visited Kawadapally in January 1975 to place the television and to fix the antenna. The village *Sarpanch* made an effort to get the television location shifted to the school, but the team did not oblige him. The antenna fixed on the roof of the community hall became an attraction. The lustrous feature of the antenna and its umbrella shape made the villagers to call it as *"Addam Lanti Chatri"* (The umbrella shaped mirror).

The anthropologist who was called as 'Television Officer' received several queries about the starting of Television. Villagers were complaining to the anthropologist about the delay in fixing the television and beginning its operations. The anthropologist tried to clarify about his role. When the deployment team visited the village for the second time in June 1975 due to absence of electric power they tested the television by connecting it to the jeep through a cable. This was a great surprise to the villagers. One of the literate young man explained that battery was being used to supply power. The children who had gathered around the television were driven away by the elders fearing they would die of electric shock. Questions were put to the team on when the programme would start, whether the *panchayat* has to bear the expenses, or any tax will be levied. The technician explained that no tax would be levied as the government wanted to telecast television programmes free. The young men, who were present during the testing, looked with surprise at the television signals being checked.

The second visit of the deployment team lead to picking up of discussion about the television. The choice of custodian operator (a non-local teacher), the location of television and the timings were the subject of discussion. Ramulamma told that the television would function in the morning for school children and in the evening for adults so that cultivators could watch the programmes. She pleaded to relocate the television away from Scheduled Castes *Jati* ward as she felt the television would be avoided by many for that reason.

Television Location

As already mentioned, the *Sarpanch* did not like the location of television. Many villagers also opined that the television would have been placed near Hanuman shrine in *Wadloni Dhatti* which was central place of the village. Members of the village, other than Scheduled Castes *Jati* expressed that the Scheduled Castes members do not keep the surroundings clean and their children were allowed to relieve themselves and urinate all-around the places. They dry skins and hides near the houses. Because of these the area near community hall emanates foul smell. The other *Jati* members also felt that it was not prestigious to sit in *Harijanwada*. Slowly these opinions got neutralized as villagers who were near to the community hall preferred it as it was nearer to them. The school was ruled out as it was away from the village.

Television Operator

The teacher who was appointed to operate the television was a bit indifferent. He received the training given by the technicians of SITE at Hyderabad. He also received pre- and post-telecast training of NCERT. The teacher entrusted the operation of television to another person who was originally selected for the purpose. This person was switching on the television sincerely on time, but on few occasions he was blamed for not operating television. The teacher used to switch off the programmes at 8.50 P.M. In the beginning and after some time he started switching off at 7.30 P.M. after the Telugu-Kannada capsule and national programme were over. In the villagers' opinion, the television should be on up to 8 P.M. as it would not cost the teacher a single penny. It was observed that often viewers said "what would go from the teacher's property if he allowed us to view the other programmes". This issue was taken up to the notice of village elders, but the teacher replied that they had instructions to switch off after national programme. A few times the teacher allowed to see certain programmes at popular request by not strictly following the timings. Power failures also sometimes caused minor problem to operate. By and large, the villagers appreciated the patience of the television operator and continuity of the operation.

The villagers preferred a teacher or a government employee to operate the television. It is opined that they will be more responsible in doing the job than a local person. Only, one or two villagers preferred a local person saying that the government employees behave in an authoritarian fashion.

Pre-SITE Viewing

The test schedule started on July 1, 1975. In the beginning, the test pattern could be viewed only on half the screen. In the second testing, two villagers came to watch the television as they learnt that SITE technicians were testing the television operations. The test schedule was switched on at 5.30 P.M., 7.30 P.M. and 9 A.M. On July 4, the first telecast was viewed (from capsules of cluster programme). The headmaster asked the viewers who had gathered around to sit and view the programme. The crowd grew in number and members of all *Jati* including children, old men and women gathered. Anxious to get a glimpse of the television, several viewers started moving close to the television without being excessively concerned about viewers of other *Jati.* First time they rubbed shoulders with many Scheduled Castes *Jati* viewers. In spite of the headmaster's efforts to bring some order, this chaos continued, even when the television screen was showing half picture. The viewers were dazzled, as for the first time they faced such brightly lit up screen.

The programme began by telecast on 'satellite launch'. The villagers were mesmerized by the new faces and objects they saw and started wondering about these objects. The anthropologists had to explain about satellite launching which facilitated them to watch the programme telecast from Ahmedabad. They felt disappointed when television programmes were put off after testing. Post-viewing discussion once again highlighted and brought the dissatisfaction about keeping the television set in *Harijanwada* apart from the shaky and bright picture shown on television. Villagers were discussing whether the shakiness could be rectified. A third aspect of discussion was about who will look after the children at home, if both husband and wife were away watching television, as they preferred to watch the television simultaneously.

Since the information about starting of television had not reached in the entire village many villagers had not joined this event. Young men, in the age group of 15-24 and 25-34 years, who were exposed to films, started making queries as they expected a lot of entertainment. The next day July 5th, villagers in the southern part of the village mildly accused the anthropologists for not informing them about the programme. On July 5th, the test pattern was seen several times and the children who saw the pattern named it as a globe.

The viewers of July 4th, differentiated the people they saw on television by saying *Manamandi Kadu* (they are not our people). The anthropologists had to intervene at this stage to clarify that the television is meant for the whole of India. One woman from the Scheduled Castes *Jati* credited her husband for impressing upon the *Sarpanch* to get the community hall constructed in their area. She said, she would try to keep the surroundings clean. On July 6th, the children arrived in the morning and informed the anthropologists that they could not see any songs or dances and not even pictures. There was only globe they said. The teacher was tense as the room was full with young viewers as soon as he had opened the community hall doors. As he could not get the picture, the youth shouted at him saying "yesterday we saw the programme when the headmaster switched on. Why are you not showing us the pictures". Meanwhile, a drummer announced about the starting of television in the whole village. More villagers gathered and there were shouts and sounds. The teacher waited for fifteen minutes and switched off the television set. It took another ten minutes for people to vacate the room. The novelty effect of television, the message spread by the drummer, and the awareness spread through word of mouth made the villagers to rush to the television in the early hours of the day. The test schedules were again telecast towards the end of July (29th, 30th and 31st). Young men from all *Jati* showed great enthusiasm to view the television. They went to the teacher's house and insisted that he should open the room and switch on the television. The adults who did not go to watch television got the information from children and youngsters.

While acknowledging that television would provide a good entertainment, a man from Gudati *Jati* expressed the opinion that work might be affected, if workers leave the fields early to watch television. On July 30th, even before the television was switched on youngsters from all *Jati* numbering about thirty waited at central place *Wadloni Dhatti* till the teacher came and followed him to the television. The women from Gudati and Gaondla *Jati* who stopped on the verandah had hesitated to go inside and sit along with male members.

Visitors from other villages also joined to watch the television. One young man of Gaondla *Jati* came from a neighbouring village to view how the television worked in Kawadapally. The viewers commented and remarked "it would be better if they (Doordarshan) showed us programmes in Telugu", "the lady announcer is good and it would be better if she comes every day". The children named the announcer as *Peddakkaish* (elder sister). It was felt that television can be kept on the verandah so that many people can view it, especially women who were feeling shy to enter the room. When it was done, they expressed satisfaction as the brightness was reduced and more people were able to watch television.

Diverse and varied opinions were expressed about the arrival of television in the village and expectations from television. The school children were keen to watch programmes on circus, science programme on atom, film on Apollo to mention a few. A literate young man opined that it would be beneficial to watch these programmes regularly. Some women were observed saying that they had to go and watch "cinema". Some youngsters felt that television should be shown around 8 pm or after 9 pm. Many elderly women said that they would be watching television even if a fee of 50 paisa was charged, but the youngsters were of the opposite view who thought they should not pay anything as there were no seating arrangements for the viewers. The elderly women reported that because there were no seats, the charge can be 50 paisa, otherwise it can be more as in cinema hall. The elders in the village showed indifference in going to *Harijanwada* to watch television.

Television and Leaders

The Police *Patel* was the first among the leaders to show inclination to see how the television looked like and how it operated. He said that he came across the news in paper and wanted to verify. He went to the television room along with a trader whom he met on the way. He tried the on and off switches and after seeing a separate meter, wanted to know who will pay the electricity tariff. He was interested in attending television inauguration in Bahadurguda village, where the Chief Minister of Andhra Pradesh was invited on the opening day. The Police *Patel* watched television for five times during the entire period of SITE. The other leaders who visited and viewed television included the Secretary of Cooperative Society from Gudati *Jati,* who came twice, the Mali *Patel* and the *Sarpanch* visited five and four times respectively. Among others, the *Panchayat* member from Abdullapurmet came just one day. Only leader in the village who watched television several times was a *Panchayat* member. Apart from these leaders, several second level leaders were viewing the television programmes occasionally. Whenever they attended their presence was being felt because of the comments they made while viewing the programme. The reasons for absence of leaders from viewing the television are as follows:

(i) These leaders visited Hyderabad almost six days in a week. They start early in the morning and return in the evening around 8.30 pm. By the time they go home and eat their dinner, the telecast used to end.

(ii) On the days the leaders were in the village, they were extremely busy.

(iii) The presence of television in the lower *Jati* section inhibited leaders to view programmes though this factor gradually became insignificant.

The *Sarpanch* preferred the location in the community hall. But other leaders felt that this location caused problems in viewing television as the Scheduled Castes *Jati* members would stand up and move, obstructing others. The leaders stopped viewing television as they did not want to make repeated request to the Scheduled Castes *Jati* members from blocking the view. The leaders however turned up promptly on special telecast days like August 15 and January 26 as they could hardly get any occasion to watch the national events taking place in Delhi.

On the other hand, the village leaders played an important role in disseminating television information which could be considered significant. For example, the *Sarpanch* was observed talking about the programmes on untouchability, agriculture and 20 point programme in the informal meetings he had with the villagers. Mali *Patel* on the other hand felt that television programme would be enriched if it was done in conjunction with a devoted extension worker who could clarify the doubts of villagers on agricultural practices. There were several telecasts which created more discussion and created difference of opinion than providing clarity. These telecast lacked common understanding.

7
Starting of Telecast

First Day of SITE

The enquiries about television increased day by day as the inauguration date approached. In the meanwhile, villagers followed with interest the inauguration of television at Bahadurpura by the Chief Minister of Andhra Pradesh. This information reached the villagers through newspapers, radio and announcements by the drummer who requested them to attend the inauguration for which lorries were arranged to transport them to Bahadurpura.

Within Kawadapally, the teachers also made arrangements for inauguration of television in the village. Youngsters (in the age group of 5-34), literate members and women were present as viewers on the first day. Children reached the television place by 5 PM itself and started playing. The youngsters too were anxious to reach the television place and managed to reach by 6 PM. It was observed that several watch wearing youngsters were keeping a tab of time to ensure timely arrival. The headmaster was surprised as none of the elders were present on the first day. The custodian operator brought a coconut, vermilion and incenses sticks. The teacher opened the room by 6:10 PM and the television was switched on. The breaking of coconut on the occasion was not carried out and the custodian took it back.

The headmaster cleared the gathering on the verandah and asked people to view television from a distance, so, that the eyes will not be affected. As soon as the signature tune started several people from all *Jati* rushed to the television place. These included relatives who came to the village from other places. The teacher arranged the children in front row so that they can view without obstruction. Three persons (one from Gudati *Jati,* two from Gaondla *Jati*) took initiative to control somewhat unruly viewers. A woman from Mustigolla *Jati* came with *Bajjis* (fried eatables) in a basket and sold them. The school teachers and literate persons acted as interpreters.

The audience included a dozen people from Abdullapurmet. The speech of the Prime Minister along with all programme was not audible due to noise created by the viewers who had gathered at the television place. Hindi language also was a problem as most of the viewers were Telugu speakers or were illiterate. The number of viewers at 6:30 PM was three hundred including about 150 children. The television custodian opined that this would be publicity for the government. The youth from Gudati *Jati* wondered after viewing an interview with the Prime Minister whether she is approachable to the people. Some viewers were found to be misinterpreting programmes. A 50 year old man from Gudati *Jati* said that television was covering more of the dances of Lambadis and even Nehru Shaib liked them and provided land and houses to them.

There was power failure twice for a few seconds. After some time, there was sound failure around 8:40 PM. The teachers decided to get the television set inside the hall by then. Three viewers from the Muslim community observed the programme carefully as they could understand Hindustani to a large extent. They were also translating programmes for other viewers. The remarkable situation was that none cared or utter issues of untouchability during viewing period though a number of Scheduled Castes *Jati* viewers sat on one side of the gathering.

Functioning of Television

The functioning of television had a definite influence on the viewing behaviour of the audience. On the first day, members expressed that frequent power failure would make them loose interest. The power break down made them to say this. The quality of picture and sound did not show much effect in the early days of novelty but slowly they had an impact. On the second day, even after volume failure there was a large gathering. But there was a lot of commotion and noise. A Scheduled Castes *Jati* member started singing and dancing which made elders from upper *Jati* to shout at him. An elderly Gaondla member wondered whether the television problems could be rectified by the doctor.

The technician of SITE from Hyderabad came on the second day and rectified the volume problem. When the technician visited the place, there was a power failure and so they were compelled to use their jeep battery. On seeing this, young man from Gudati *Jati* commented that there must be a generator in the village so that they will not miss any television programme in case of power failure. After rectification of volume problem, the audience strength started increasing in numbers from the next day.

Whenever there was some defect or power failure, the audience strength dropped the next day. This was partly due to disappointment and partly due to ignorance about the temporary nature of the problem. In fact, many houses in the neighbourhood belonging to community houses did not have electricity. Many of the regular viewers stopped viewing television during February 1976, when the power supply was restored after a brief period of disconnection of electricity due to non-payment of tariff. This occurred as the bills did not reach the *Sarpanch* and were lying with the teacher. Viewers' strength dropped in July 1976 also, when there was some disturbance in the power connection. Once the defect was rectified, it took two days to get the usual audience strength.

The one year analysis of power supply and its negative effects on attendance of viewers was a major lesson that should be rectified for regular attendance of the viewers.

Climate Conditions and Television Viewing

The viewing behaviour of audience was also affected by the climatic conditions of the place. The audience strength got reduced from the range of 250-300 to 100-150 range by the end of August. This was because day light was available till 7 PM in August, though, sunset was at around 6:30 PM. Cultivators were continuing in fields as long as there was light and returned home after night fall. This inhibited the viewers from attending television telecast. During rainy season also audience strength came down because of slushy conditions and fear of snakes which were moving around looking for frogs. During rainy season, those who were undertaking strenuous operations like ploughing during the daytime preferred television viewing in the night. In the rainy season, the television was kept inside the room instead of verandah and the small size of the room and lack of cleanliness, tanning odour also affected the size. The audience size further reduced in September and October as winter affected size of the audience. The children strength was reduced during December and January. In February, the children component reached its original size after rise of temperature. March again showed a downward trend due to marriage season and the toddy tapping operations of Gaondla. In summer months, average audience size fluctuated from 142 to 114 and 121 during April, May and June. July again saw a decline due to frequent rains and power breakdowns. By and large, rainy season affected the audience size, along with occupational seasons which also showed some affect.

Occupational Season and Television Viewing

The Anthropologist maintained daily diary of audience attendance to record the audience size. Based on the analysis of the audience, the efforts were made to relate occupational season and television viewing behaviour. The whole SITE year can be divided into (i) peak occupational season and (ii) slack occupational season. Table 7.1 gives the seasons, works and average audience size. The seasons clearly reflect the agricultural cycle followed in the village like other Telangana villages having multiple cropping pattern followed in the village, interwoven with the Hindu calendrical system. It can be observed from the analysis that Kawadapally is a multi-cropping village and farmers follow the agriculture cycle very closely.

As can be seen from Table 7.1, cropping seasons have their effects on audience strength. Audience strength increased whenever there were festivals in Kawadapally as other villagers also joined audience. Male, female ratio also was affected due to seasons. During ploughing season more males were absent. During toddy tapping season Gaondla male strength declined.

Television Timings and Audience Strength

Television timings also influenced viewers' strength. Adult

Table 7.1: Seasonal Agriculture Operations and Audience Size during SITE

Sl. No.	*Month*	*Local Season*	*Operations*	*Average Audience Size*
1.	Second week of May	Katteralu Karti	Ploughing in wet lands for paddy nursery (Kattera wadulu)	144
2.	Last week of May	Rohini Karti	Ploughing of dry land waiting for monsoon to sow *jowar*, *bajra*	
3.	First half of June	Mrigam karte	Transplantation of paddy (Kattera wadulu), groundnut sowing and plouging late sowing of *jowar* and *bajra*	121
4.	Second half of June	Ardra karte	Ploughing for castor seeds, if there is rain weeding in *jowar* and *bajra*	
5.	First half of July	Pedda pushyalu karte	Paddy nursery weeding ploughing for castor, weeding operations in *jowar* and *bajra*	90
6.	Second half of July	China Pushyalu	Sowing castor, weeding in *jowar* and *bajra*	
7.	First half of August	Aslerlu	Castor sowing, weeding operations	100
8.	Second half of August	Makha	Completion of castor sowing. Harvest of Kattera wadulu (paddy) starts	
9.	First half of September	Pubba	Completion of Kattera paddy weeding in groundnut and castor	85
10.	Second half of September	Uttara	Sowing of horsegram transplantation of Sambalu paddy. Threshing and completion of late Kattera wadulu.	

(*Contd.*)

Table 7.1: (*Contd.*)

Sl. No.	*Month*	*Local Season*	*Operations*	*Average Audience Size*
11.	Last week of September to first week of October	Harstha	Jowar, Bajra and groundnut harvest, transplantation of sambalu paddy	90
12.	Second to third week of October	Chitta	Late sambalu paddy transplantation occasional weeding of castor	
13.	Last week of October to first week of November	Swati	Dussera and Diwali festivals	133
14.	Rest of November	Visakha and Anuradha	Irrigation and looking after paddy nursery	
15.	December	Jyestha and Moola	Early transplantation of second crop	100
16.	January	Purvashadha Uttarashadha	Continuation of transplantation for second crop start of harvest in castor	96
17.	February	Sravanam Dhanista	Irrigation and weeding second crop paddy, transplantation in wet land of Sambalu. Marriage season starts	184
18.	March	Phalugnam	Starting of harvest of second crop, marriage season in full swing. Visiting of friends and relatives	102
19.	April	Chaitram	Visit of relatives, Ugadi Sri Ramanavami festivals. Transporting manure to fields	142

component increased with late timings. Both adult workers and housewives appreciated late timings as they were able to finish their work without hurrying. The best time for adults was after 7:30 PM. Child audience increased mostly in summer months.

Those Watching Television

As long as the novelty effect was there, it used to be a large audience. After August, the strength reduced resulting in a consolidated core audience. Towards the end names of hundred individuals who had 60 per cent audience attendance were listed out by the anthropologists. Out of this 100, six persons watched television throughout the year. They belonged to the age group of 15-24 years. Among these, two were students, of which one was a student who had failed his examination; two apprentice toddy tappers and one cultivator were present. Viewers who were watching television for 9 months included four women in the age group of 25-44 years.

Factors Affecting Television Viewing

The villagers residing in the southern part of the village had been observed to watch television less number of times. Those who were having their work location towards northern end of the village have maintained 60 per cent attendance at viewing. This could be because the television was located on the north side of the village. The female viewers were drawn largely from the age group of 15-24 and above 35 years. The female members of *Patel* Khandan, *Patwari* Khandan viewed television only as novelty. The daughter-in-laws of Pedda Goudu also avoided viewing television as they were expected to show respect to the elder members of their in-law's *inteperu* (surname) group. The female viewers comprised mostly mothers-in-law and unmarried females. These restrictions were less in Scheduled Castes *Jati* households.

Festivals, deaths and marriage seasons directly influenced the audience strength. In case of a death, the audience did not come to watch television but instead gathered around the deceased body. In one case elders told the custodian not to switch on the television. During marriage season in March, the viewers' strength dropped to 102 while it was 184 in February and 142 in April. But actually during death and marriage occasions, the audience strength used to fluctuate because of arrival of relatives from non-SITE villages. The audience strength touched lowest on festivals like *Rama navami jatra, Sassara, Bonalu Panduga* and *Peerla Panduga. Veera Bhadra Swami Jatra* in neighbouring Balijagudem village also affected the viewers as the custodian went there ignoring his television duty. Those who had assembled to watch television on that day did not protest and a few also proceeded towards Balijagudem.

Programme Preferences

The programme preferences were carried out on the basis of individual interviews of the viewers and observations during viewing by the anthropologists. It was observed that the television programmes that were interesting were watched by the viewers without any interruption or disturbances. On the other hand, the prorgrammes considered uninteresting were not viewed attentively. During the telecast the viewers' got involved in chit chat and gossip while ignoring the viewing. The interesting programmes post viewing also attracted discussions, analysis and explanation. Villagers entering the television location in a hurry also indicated their preferences to watch programmes. Programme preferences have been discussed under two headings.

A. School Programme: Children in the age group of 5-8 years (Standard I and II) preferred programme which had movement and action. They did not like static and lecture type of viewing and they were involved in their own activity during such programmes. Interest in audio apart from video had increased from standard 3 to 5. These children liked songs and stories with content, not just the action and the movement. Elder students were trying to catch and repeat some of the songs and words. Thus, the preferences of programme varied between different classes.

B. Evening Programme: The evening programmes were classified by the viewers into *aata pata* (entertainment) and *Batuku teru Sangati* (Information on livelihood). The former being entertainment and the later being instructional. Among instructional programmes, agricultural programmes which the viewers termed as *vyavasayam sangati* were preferred. They felt that these programmes will educate them and bring awareness and those who can afford can practice them. After the closure of

SITE many of the informants recalled more agriculture, animal husbandry and nutrition programmes than entertainment and other programmes. With regard to entertainment programmes, villagers showed interest to find out whether or not they will be in Telugu. Among entertainment programmes, the best liked are *Oggu Katha, Burra Katha, Hari Katha* and Dramas. The Dramas having both mythological and social themes received applause from the audience. Thus folk ballads and dramas were not preferred among entertainment programmes.

Programmes and Responses

Instructional programmes can be categorized into (i) agriculture, animal husbandry and poultry farming; (ii) health, hygiene and nutrition; (iii) family planning; (iv) primary education; and (v) national integration. Of these, five categories primary education programmes were telecast during morning period. Educational programmes meant for adults comprised of items like community matters, general knowledge, developmental activities and improved appliances. Table 7.2 shows the distribution of all the programmes telecast during SITE according to their broad area/ content.

Agriculture

Majority of the agricultural programmes consisted of information on improved methods of cultivation. Over two dozen programmes of the type were telecast during SITE. Programmes on tips while planting rice were repeated six times. Programmes on crops like cotton, sunflower, sugarcane and maize which are not grown in Kawadapally were also watched. Viewers were discussing about these and were recalling names of other places (villages) where these crops were grown. A couple of cultivators who once cultivated sunflower revealed that they could not get enough yield and the oil were not relished by them. Programmes on farm equipment were watched with mixed reaction. Viewers mentioned that they were watching some of the equipments for the first time except for the hand compressor sprayer. A teacher having his own agriculture field tried to enquire about seed drill and paddy puddler after learning about their prices. Not being able to locate them either in the block office or in city market, the teacher started telling villagers that the equipment being shown on television are those newly developed by the agricultural university. Programmes on available equipment like sprayers received much appreciation whereas non-availability of equipment affected the credibility of television message.

Table 7.2: Distribution of Programmes according to Content/Broad Area of Andhra Pradesh and Karnataka Clusters

Sl. No.	*Content/Broad Area of Programmes*	*Total Number of Programmes*		*Total Exposure (with repetitions)*	
		No.	%	No.	%
1.	Agriculture	45	5.1	90	7.3
2.	Animal Husbandry	27	3.1	43	3.5
3.	Family Planning	50	5.7	68	5.5
4.	Health, Hygiene and Nutrition	88	10	145	11.8
5.	National Integration	25	2.8	38	3.1
6.	Institutional Items (other than SITE objectives)	79	9.0	93	7.5
7.	20 Point Economic Programme	79	9.0	106	8.6
8.	Emergency Propaganda	26	2.9	30	2.4
9.	Miscellaneous Information Programmes	58	6.6	61	5.0
10.	Films Division Documentaries including Indian News Review	92	10.5	106	8.6
11.	Entertainment				
	(i) Telugu	95	10.8	139	11.3
	(ii) Kannada	95	10.8	157	12.7
	(iii) Other Languages	60	6.8	74	6.0
12.	Children Programmes				
	(i) Telugu	30	3.4	48	3.9
	(ii) Kannada	30	3.4	34	2.8
	Total	**879**	**100.0**	**1232**	**100.0**

There were sometimes distortions of messages too. A viewer from neighbouring village, in the course of discussions on farm equipment, observed that because of introduction of machines that can replace traditional cattles used in farming, the cattle wealth is declining. The viewer was of the view that increased slaughtering of cattles has led to price rise as a large number of cattle are being sent to the slaughter houses. This could be because the viewer happened to be cattle trader and broker.

The information on inputs like fertilizers and compost were already known to the villagers and viewers recalled various aspects of these. One person, who was trained in developing compost pit but who had not shared this knowledge with others, recalled this information received by him. There are two others (one from Gudati *Jati* and other from Mustigolla *Jati)* who showed interest for compost pits but their enthusiasm did not last long.

About a dozen programmes on different kinds of insects were shown. Viewers responded favourably to the programme on semi-looper on castor. Castor is grown in large quantity in Kawadapally and this accounted for the enthusiasm. The programme on stem borer on paddy had made inroads into the knowledge of the cultivators. Some of them examined their crop, found it affected by the pest and sprayed Eldrin (insecticide) as suggested on television. Several other programmes received appreciation of the villagers, but were not taken seriously as crops like mango and cotton were not grown by them.

The response of the viewers differed about spurious pesticides, fertilizers and safe use of pesticides among different sections of farmers. A few literate young farmers from Gudati *Jati* expressed happiness that they now would be able to identify genuine pesticides and fertilizers from spurious ones. With regard to safe use of insecticides, there was indifference as viewers expressed that it is not convenient to follow all the precautions like using apron, covering the mouth with a cloth etc. A few young farmers opined that these are better methods. The younger generation is prone to change whereas older generation looked at things with indifference.

Certain special programmes on agricultural operations were telecast during May, June 1976 for few cultivators as they were busy preparing their land for coming season. Many of these programmes, being repetitions, did not arouse much interest among viewers.

The analysis of agricultural programmes was indicative of selective acceptance of innovative practices that were practical and considered useful by the farmers. At the same time, several programmes like precautions to be taken on safe use of insecticides were ignored.

Animal Husbandry

Programmes covering cattle, poultry, sheep, pig and fish rearing were telecast once in a week during entire SITE period. There were also special serialized telecasts during January and May 1976 on poultry farming and various cattle diseases.

Programmes on growing fodder crops for milch cattle and using foliage of crops like sunflower were received with indifference. There were humorous comments like why do not they (Government) give the farmers those tractors so that the farmers can also grow crop in larger areas. Some of these messages were further disseminated to non-viewers when the viewers met and interacted in places like irrigation wells. These messages however remained incomplete or partial leading to no effective adoption of the messages.

Programmes on calf rearing, maintenance of cattle sheds, cross-breeding of cows, first aid to cattle had been watched with interest. Viewers familiar with cross-breeds recalled their knowledge. Feeding calves with bottled milk surprised the viewers. They also did not relish the idea of arresting the growth of horns. They felt the beauty of the animal will be lost. These two messages reached many non-viewers. After viewing programme on cross-breeds some viewers expressed though in lighter vein that like small farmers (having small quantities of land) those owning small cattle also should be given loans. There was willingness to acquire better quality cattle if sufficient capital was available.

While viewing poultry programme, there were discussions on the poultry farms present on the highway to Hyderabad city. They felt that one should take poultry farming as full time job if the money and expertise were available. The programme on sheep rearing was watched with interest but was not discussed further. This is because sheep rearing is taken up traditionally by *Jati* like Kurma Sakanati and Yerra of the Gaondla *Jati* cluster.

Special serial programmes on cattle diseases were telecast during May 1976. The messages received immediate attention and got a good amount of circulation. The cattle owners reacted in mentioning about the diseases they reported to the veterinary hospital and vaccinations done. The viewers also criticized the veterinary doctor and compounder for performing their duties properly. Though the programmes were appreciated, limited change in the attitudes and practices was found. When an epidemic broke out one viewer from the core audience took initiative to pool contributions for inviting a *Mantragadu* (magician healer) to propitiate the goddess responsible for the outbreak of epidemic. Some young farmers informed the veterinary doctor through the police *patel* and a compounder was sent from the dispensary. Those who paid their contributions to *Mantragadu* also got their cattle inoculated. They justified this by saying that one should try all methods to stop the outbreak of epidemic. They fear that *Mantragadu* is capable of directing epidemic on their cattle, if contributions were not paid. Viewers were not hesitant to approach the veterinary doctor if the traditional technique of treatment were not effective. There was awareness about vaccinations and inoculations prior to television programme, but the telecasts made younger people become more vocal about the competence of modern medicine.

Family Planning

Programmes on family planning were being telecast once in a week. Of the various programmes, the discussions and interviews on family planning were not followed keenly by the viewers. They were sitting away from the television in small groups until the next entertainment programme was telecast. However, the dramas, ballads and dances having family planning theme were watched with interest. During these programmes viewers were discussing how government is conveying family planning message through all possible media. The viewers were also seen discussing the desirability of having small family as the lands could not grow, but the number of children who would claim a share on the land would increase.

Another area of family planning that was keenly discussed beyond television programme telecast related to loss of virility and physical human strength due to family planning operation. Some of the women mentioned how their in-laws prevented them from undergoing tubectomy. Discussion among village adults clearly indicated that the messages on family planning helped reinforce the existing knowledge of the viewers and made them arguelogically. Economic considerations are important for the people. If one is convinced that his work will not suffer because of family planning operation, it will be accepted. Fear of complications is another factor which needs to be removed. Some of the viewers were quite willing to undergo operations, if they received assurance about lack of complications.

Health, Hygiene and Nutrition

Under this area, majority of the programmes were on nutrition. Health programmes centred on diseases, treatment and prevention. Telecast of programmes on hygiene were fewer in number and focused on themes like 'drinking water'.

Telecast of health programmes provided information on extension personnel, hospitals and preventive measures. The programmes on health extension personnel made the viewers critical of the functioning of local doctors, health visitor and primary health centre. They compared these with what was shown on television. They opined that the health visitor who visits once in a month and signs on the walls should come more frequently. Telecast on leprosy, malaria, conjunctivitis, TB, night blindness were watched with rapt attention. Programme on leprosy led to distortion by one individual due to the lack of clear pronunciation. Leprosy which is known as *Khustu* in Telugu was considered as something to do with devotees of Krishna. Telecast on whopping cough had been recalled when a small girl was suffering from severe cough. The term carrot was not understood when it was stated in the programme on night blindness. The programme on Rabies made the children kill a stray dog which was suspected to be affected with rabies. The viewers were aware that mosquitoes were responsible for spread of malaria. The word 'polio' was heard by 99 per cent of the audience for the first time. They were ignorant of polio vaccine and triple antigen. On the whole, the programmes made the audience aware of prevention and cure of various diseases and enhanced their knowledge.

The impact of these health telecast was limited and even after watching these telecast some villagers avoided vaccination and continued worship of *Pochamma,* a goddess considered to be responsible for epidemic diseases. The programme on drinking water made the viewers aware of the cleanliness to be maintained at various sources of drinking water. The viewers were discussing about the tapeworm menace which they faced till recently. The awareness had not altered their practices as many ruled out the possibility of adopting some of the measures which were time consuming and need re-education of housewives.

The nutrition programmes were on children's diet, to enhance the nutritive values of the food and preparation of new food items. The supplementary diets for children like making groundnut biscuits, tomato juice and eggs received mixed attention. Viewers opined that various new food items could be prepared only by housewives of upper *Jati* like Brahmin and Komati as they had necessary leisure time. Though, it was agreed that food prepared with new methods should be more nutritive, the viewers were doubtful about the taste. They also mentioned that they could not afford the fruits which were part of various items on nutrition. One woman from Gaondla *Jati* who sold vegetables in the village started telling others to buy tomatoes and green vegetables so that they could become strong as telecast on the television. By and large, the analysis of nutrition telecast tended to support the view that the knowledge level of the viewers had considerably increased due to television viewing of nutrition programme.

National Integration

The programmes on national integration brought about awareness beyond their village and region and outside world. Television viewing allowed exposure to and presence of various religions, languages and regions of the country and in the process the viewers became aware of multilingual India. The programmes on national integration expanded the horizon of the people beyond their *Rajyam* (state or province) which is within a radius of 40 km. They also started repeating several new words shown on television.

8

Television, Primary Education and Teacher's Training

One of the major components of SITE was telecast of primary education for school children in the age group of 5-12 years. Since this segment was an important objective of the SITE it was dealt separately for which educational planners of National Council of Educational Research and Training (NCERT), New Delhi were directly involved and collaborated on SITE. In this section efforts will be made to highlight and analyse the findings of primary education telecast and its effect on primary education.

Primary Education

The 'Tele School' as it was called was showing programmes on primary education in the morning time for 22 and 1/2 minutes on all school working days. Once in a week science programmes produced by Space Applications Centre, Ahmedabad were telecast. Though the visual techniques of these programmes received applaud from the children, the audio part was not effective due to faulty dubbing from Hindi to Telegu and bad Telugu commentary. The age of the children affected their comprehension and ability to recall. Age of the children studying in class 1-5 showed a great deal of variation in their level of programme comprehension. It was observed that the children in lower classes (class 1 and 2) could not recall, or recalled a very limited number of visuals; children from higher classes (class 4 and 5) were able to recall the programmes entirely. Programmes depicting the making of dolls and objects with paper and clay attracted the children most.

Students even attempted making many of the items telecast on television. These 'do it yourself' programmes brought their urge to learn new things as well as enhance their inherent skills to flower, especially among older children from higher classes. Several educative programmes like visits to the cities, tourist places, and industrial areas were viewed with uninterrupted silence and many of these were recalled in the later interviews. They even noted down some of the songs. The animal series of ISRO which is partly educative and partly entertaining had been the best recalled programme by all children.

Participation of Teachers

As apart of this programme short term training to selected primary school science teachers were organized twice for a period of two weeks during holidays. State Council of Educational Research and Training was responsible for the training of teachers in which pre- and post-television viewing was made a mandatory activity. The teachers who underwent this training did not show interest in performing the task. The Headmaster of the school showed some enthusiasm in asking questions on the programmes viewed by students. The teachers felt that new teaching methods shown on television are highly useful for them in teaching but were doubtful whether they can be put into practice. Since the training was focused primarily for science teachers, it required demonstration, field observations and resources to carry out the experiments. However, it was felt by the trainee teachers that they would not be able to follow them due to lack of space in the classroom, necessary teaching aids and shortage of teachers. At the same time, it was observed that during post-demonstration period, resources were available in the village while following methods in teaching Botany. However, teachers looked at new methods as a burden that increased their responsibilities without any monetary gain.

Educational Programmes (in the evening)

Programmes on organizations like N.C.C., fire fighting, home guards and civil defense were viewed with interest. Viewers mistook some of them as military programme. Viewers made enquiries about *gobar* gas plants after watching them on television.

Information on social services like N.S.S. institutions and industries were viewed with interest, but there was no further dissemination of information. Physical training programmes like *yogabhyasa* attracted many and some even made an attempt to practice. The message reached non-viewers that a *Pahalwan* (wrestler) was performing acrobatics. Games like *Kabaddi* and Volleyball were viewed with interest. Programmes on post office, banks and other service organizations led to criticism on their functioning in the village and surrounding area. These programmes brought awareness about facilities and amenities available to the public and their proper use. Messages are observed to be passed on to non-viewers on programmes with a good Telugu commentary. Films Division documentaries served a lot as they provided a good commentary.

Telecast of such programmes were useful to create awareness among the viewers, but due to lack of support they were either misunderstood or not taken seriously.

Programme on Women

Most of the programmes on women were attacking the local cultural practices and were rejected by the viewers. Making of various items like dolls and embroidery also did not evoke much response as the average women in the village opined that they had no time for these leisure time activities. Programmes on destitute homes, social welfare homes and other amenities for women were viewed with indifference. The rice cookers that were shown were alien to most of the women so was the practice of serving hot rice.

Emergency and 20 Point Economic Programme

About 11 per cent of the total Andhra Pradesh/ Karnataka segment programmes were telecast on 20 point programme and the national state of emergency that was imposed during the telecast period of one year and beyond by the then Prime Minister of India. As a part of 20 point programme, the programmes were telecast related to moratorium on rural debts. Such programmes brought uneasiness among the rich as it advocated that the poor need not repay their loans. Further, the programme on 20 point plan aroused indifference among rich landlords while bringing hope, conflicts and frustration among poor farmers and labourers.

Programmes in Other Languages

Programmes in other languages on agriculture and entertainment received good appreciation. News was not liked by the audience. It was observed that most of the viewers were indifferent towards Hindi news and were involved in chit chat and gossip when news was telecast from Delhi. Weather bulletin attracted the literates who could understand Hindustani. Words like *Samachar, Namaskar* entered the vocabulary of the youngsters.

Entertainment

The children's programmes telecast on every Sunday were attended by a large number of adults also. The villagers identified Sunday programme as complete entertainment. The Hindi movies which were shown in the Hindi cluster programme were another attraction on last Sunday of every month. Among other entertainment programmes, dramas of mythological and historical themes were popular. Social dramas on themes such as dowry, corruption and child marriages were appreciated. All these were further disseminated to non-viewers. One of the dramas related to moratorium on rural loans was discussed for weeks in the village and was recalled much later. Dances and songs based on light music received more appreciation than the classical ones. The audience which used to be around 150 to 200 during a preceding Telugu programme was coming down to 30 or even less for an Urdu entertainment programme. Folk items like *Burrakatha, Oggukatha, Golla Suddula* were always welcomed by the villagers and were subjected to further dissemination.

Dissemination of Information

The children after viewing the programmes in the morning and evening passed the details to their grandparents. They were found telling their parents especially only when asked for it. Some of the items like pottery making were found to be of subject for communication in the *Jati* interested in the item like *Kummari* (potter). Discussions were also observed among *Jati* members at their work places like Blacksmith's workshop. Communication was also taking place beyond the village boundaries through special visits. Daughters visiting their parents in Kawadapally were also carrying back information on certain messages to their in-laws houses.

Doordarshan in Kawadapally

Nearly after ten years gap television viewing was back in Kawadapally. From 1986-87 onwards Kawadapally witnessed proliferation in the number of television sets. In 1975-76, there was only SITE television present in the village for a limited period whereas the eighties saw television sets being added one by one. The first ones to acquire television was rich Gudati *Jati* landlord, followed by the Gaondla (toddy tappers). At the time of re-study, the total number of television sets present in the village was 40 including one colour television and a portable set. It is interesting to note that of these 40 households possessing television sets, thirty also had radio sets of different types. The presence of television sets among different *Jati* households is shown in Table 8.1.

Table 8.1: *Jati*-wise Distribution of Television Sets

Name of the Jati	*Number of Households Owning Television Sets*
Gudati	17
Gaondla	10
Komati	3
Padma Sali	3
Musilm	2
Kammari, Kamsali, Erukula Golla and Katika	1 each *5 = 5
Total	**40**

The Gudati *Jati* households possessed maximum number of television sets in the village. The Gaondla *Jati* who had become prosperous because of toddy business, come next to Gudati *Jati*. Others who posses television sets were traders, employees and other occupational specialists. Significant number of television owners belongs to landless and small farmer category (Table 8.1).

This indicates the growing importance of non-agricultural activities in the village economy.

Those who are employees, self-employed or cultivators having subsidiary source of earning were found to own television sets more than compared to mere cultivators. This was evident from the occupations of television owners, *viz.*, toddy tappers, toddy contractors, *kirana* (provision) shopkeepers, vegetable vendors, weavers, carpenters, blacksmiths, cloth merchants, tailors, and poultry owners, employees in school, road transport corporation workers and theater operators. All important leaders in the village like *Sarpanch, Patwari* and other important figures owned the television. A look at the educational status of the television owners revealed that 10 of them studied up to high school and above, 5 up to primary level and 11 were from elementary school level. Rest were non-literates. After the unprecedented expansion of satellite television in private sector it would be difficult to indicate the exact number of television owners in the village.

Table 8.2: Distribution of Television Sets

Land Ownership Category	*Number of Television Sets*
Landless	19
Up to 2 acres	6
3 to 5 acres	5
6 to 10 acres	4
11 to 15 acres	1
16 to 20 acres	4
21 to 25 acres	1
Total	**40**

Preferences in Doordarshan Viewing

By the time of the re-study television had become part of the daily life in Kawadapally. Eighty four respondents said that they watched television at some time or other. Another fifteen said that they watched television on specific days like Saturday, Sunday and Friday. Morning transmission meant for children (tele school) was not popular. Only two respondents said they switched on the television in the mornings whenever they were free. Afternoon transmission also was not popular during the time of study because of language problem and inconvenient timing. The following programmes were being watched by respondents in the descending order of the number of viewers. Telugu film (99), Telugu film songs (54), Telugu news (53), serials (40), plays (19), agricultural programmes (16), sports (2), tele school (2), UGC programmes and health programmes were mentioned by one individual each. It is clear that recreational and entertainment programmes were most preferred. Agricultural programmes came in distant next. When probed further respondents told that they watched agricultural programmes just because they happen to be telecast during their free time. The programmes were viewed because they were the ones which were telecast when they reached home. Majority of the viewers in the village watched television between 6:30 PM to 8:30 PM. The general pattern of transmission during that period included agricultural programmes, serials, news, plays and film songs and discussions. Few viewers were watching television between 5:30 PM to 6:30 PM and 8:30 PM to 9:30 PM. Nobody reported watching television after 9:30 PM.

Viewers preferred Telegu (regional) Kendra transmission from Hyderabad over Delhi transmission. The programmes watched from Delhi Kendra were serials like *Ramayana, Mahabharata* and *Tipu Sultan,* apart film songs and news. Among the serials and plays in Telugu those having social themes were preferred, which were followed by historical and popular folklore themes. Special telecasts like cricket matches were well known to the children of Kawadapally and they were familiar with the names of cricket players. During the study period, once a children team from Abdullapurmet came to Kawadapally to play cricket. The match was abandoned in the middle due to disputed umpiring decision. Saturday evening, the villagers gather around the television set to watch Telugu movie (now the movie is shown on Sunday). It is observed that mostly on this day, those who did not have television sets visited their relatives and friends houses for watching television. Working relationship and physical proximity played an important role than *Jati* relationship in allowing television viewers for film viewing. The popularity of the films can also be seen in some of the cases where video movies were being watched frequently. A video cassette player was hired from Abdullapurmet for this purpose.

Television Advertisements

The advertisements being shown on television were popular with all age groups and more so with children. Children were able to recall details of advertisements though they were currently not being telecast on television. Most well remembered advertisements were on washing powders, tooth pastes, soaps, tea, popular medicines, clothes, cloth soaps, fertilizers, shampoos, health drinks and two wheelers. In response to advertisements and its effects while buying advertised products the answers were as follows:

(1) "We buy what is necessary"; we buy what is available; we want to buy many of them but there is no money; we are not able to understand what is shown and the items shown are not meant for us.

Villagers' Perception of Television Impact

Villagers in general opined that there was more sophistication and awareness because of television especially among younger generations that was viewed as positive change. Children were more active and thoughtful as they were copying what was shown on television. Other positive changes include growing awareness on health and cleanliness. Urban attire was more in demand among all *Jati* children who preferred to wear pants and shirts (by boys) and Punjabi dresses (*salwar kurta* by girls). The elders perceived these changes as if it was a dramatic difference and compared them as between earth and sky when compared to earlier days. There was visible change in the dialect spoken and youngsters were speaking in '*shany*' (Suhani in Hindi) manner. Hair styles, usage of cosmetics and washing habits had become popular. It was also observed that there was increased awareness about immunization, natal care, and nutrition, fuel saving methods, savings and earnings. Villagers were seen discussing the Doordarshan news, especially the political affairs. During the fieldwork period, a topic which was under debate was the Gulf war and the role of United States of America (USA). The young children seemed to know about impeding 1990 Census that was acquired from viewing television programmes. The male viewers pointed that there was something for women to spend their leisure due to television shows. The responses of villagers on the changes brought about by television seemed to be positive and welcoming.

As can be seen from Table 8.3, majority of those who replied to the questions perceived as positive changes due to television viewing along with few negative changes (Table 8.3).

Table 8.3: Changes Occurring Due to Television Viewing

Positive Changes	74
Negative Changes	13
Positive and Negative Changes	2
No Change/Superficial Change	20
No Idea/No time/Don't watch	8
Other Responses (Complaints and Suggestions)	6
No Response	99

Negative Impact of Television by 1991

Those who perceived negative changes in the village opined that youngsters were getting spoiled by viewing television. According to them, the children were wasting their time on watching television, even on programmes they were not supposed to watch. Agriculture activities, schooling and other domestic works seemed to be neglected as children were watching cricket. Girls were getting new ideas by watching love stories on television. Because of education and watching the love stories they often refused to arrange marriages. Similarly, children were imitating cinema action and fashion. Many of them have started addressing their parents as 'Mummy' and 'Daddy'. The women seem to have empowered themselves and insisted on their rights. It seemed elders were not getting their due respect as in the past. Many consumables which were considered unnecessary were being purchased because of television advertisements.

Some elders opined that increased awareness and exposure had led to spoiling the working relation between *Jatis*. A rich Gudati *Jati* landlord complained that "now even *Dalits* have to be addressed properly and the lower *Jati* no longer listen to us". He pointed out that high daily wages were demanded and even then they were not willing to work. He says "now labourers prefer city work than labour in the fields". It was further reported that the daily wage workers in the city had limited hours to work whereas in the village these daily wage workers were expected to work for the entire day. Also city provided several attractions that were not in the village. Gudati *Jati* landlord further pointed out that though they were paying less wages compared to city, but then they were offering a number of fringe benefits to the workers. Traditional work benefited all as the rich man was like a tree and provided shadow to all those who came to him. Now, it was no longer the same. Now, daily wage workers preferred to commute to the city in search of work neglecting the available work in the village".

The above perception of a rich landlord reveals the rising expectations of workers and the consequent situation in the sphere of inter-*Jati* relations.

During the second fieldwork, it was felt that *Dalits,* on the other hand, in the village did not see any improvement in their position. They felt that they continued to be discriminated by other *Jatis*. They did not have television sets and majority did not watch television. The information awareness they felt was mostly due to oral interpersonal communication and *Jati* level communication but not due to television viewing.

One major difference between SITE television and Doordarshan was the restricted access to television of Doordarshan programmes due to growing individual ownership. Quite a few *Jatis* did not have a single television set in the houses of their *Jati* members. Television viewing depended on the proximity of households having television set and the mutual relations between the households who owned television and allowed neighbours to view the television.

In the changed circumstances viewers gathering in the individual homes largely consisted of young and one or two old viewers. More than the *Jati,* it was the working relations and neighbourhood contacts which were important in allowing outsiders to watch television. Availability of space in the television room was one major limiting factor. Presence of male members of the household also was an inhibiting factor for neighbourhood females interested in viewing television. Meal timings in the household also prevented the visiting viewers in few households.

Memories of SITE Television

Elderly members still remembered SITE television as the first television that came to the village. Some of them thought that

M.V.T. Raju had brought television to the village. Old timers were unanimous in accepting that the SITE television set was much larger when compared to present day television sets. They remembered with nostalgia the days when the whole village used to gather at one place in the evening for television viewing. Agricultural labour used to insist that they be left from the work by 5:00 PM, so, that they can watch television especially on Sundays when the film was telecast. In those days, the viewers used to get together for viewing television and often waited in anticipation of starting the television. They also sought clarification and held discussions along with several common grievances like power failure and late switching of television by the custodian. It provided the viewers time for common activity for all the *Jati* near television set. The SITE television set was a mark of pride for the village as it was not there in many other villages. Now, the poorer households complained that the upper *Jati* television owners did not allow them to view television. They called SITE television as poor man's television whereas present television was for those who had money. They said that had the SITE television been there, nobody could have prevented them from viewing.

It is generally agreed that SITE television showed more agricultural and educational programmes. Individuals remembered the different kinds of ploughs that were shown cattle rearing methods, new techniques of pottery making and health programmes. Entertainment programmes like films, *burrakathas, butta baghavatham* and plays were remembered. Items like *Uttar Gograhanam, Tablu-Kundelu* (Tortoise and Rabbit) and old films starring A. Nageshwara Rao as hero were mentioned. Plays showing atrocities and discrimination against *Harijans* were also mentioned. News was the least remembered of all programmes shown on SITE television.

Looking back at SITE days those who now owned television were happy that the telecasts were available for longer duration with more coverage in Telugu and the picture quality was better. According to these viewers now good films were being telecast frequently and also there were regular telecast of films songs. There was more variety now and also more news. Agricultural programmes telecast were fewer though advertising was more and attractive. There was private viewing of video. In the process radio started losing its importance in the village. Many viewers were of the opinion that television viewing had increased sophistication and village development.

Though SITE television exposed the villagers to several innovations, the villagers could not take advantage of what they had learnt due to lack of proper infrastructure and guidance to experiment or attempt. Though in many instances, the villagers accepted the efficacy of what was shown on television, they had no opportunity to try them on their own. Those who watched SITE television still remembered quite a few programmes that they had watched. They felt that unless government provides those necessary equipments and assistance, they would not be able to follow television recommendations. Similar opinions were expressed during 1991 by one educated cultivator who pointed out that the same was true for Doordarshan telecast in which several innovative practices in agriculture and animal husbandry were telecast, but development personnel were neither enthusiastic nor equipped for assistance.

SITE and Doordarshan: An Overview Picture

Villagers of Kawadapally first saw television programmes during SITE (1975-76). Television in those days was an innovation and a sort of craze among certain sections of the village population. Television viewing happened to be a village affair and viewers used to get together in evening at the building where the television set was located. Women folk and labourers attended adjusting the timings of their household chores and work timings. The presence of the school teacher, television operator cum custodian and the anthropologist helped to clarify about many issues villagers saw for the first time on television. Television increased their awareness and development consciousness especially amongst progressive villagers. A variety of programmes were shown as part of SITE where the emphasis was more on educational and awareness programmes than entertainment. Occupational seasons, climatic conditions and social factors affected the audience strength. The message conveyed by the television programmes were further disseminated at work spots, gossip centres and through kin and other social interactions. Though the television was located in the *Harijanwada,* it could draw audience from all social groups of the village after some initial reservations. The villagers and especially the youngsters experienced a sort of vacuum after one year of SITE. Villagers tried to adopt development innovations they had seen on SITE telecasts, whenever possible. This was true especially of those from younger generation. It was nearly after ten years from discontinuation of SITE telecast, television sets made their appearance on the village scene. By that time villagers were already aware of Doordarshan which they had been watching in Hyderabad city at different places. Though television sets were added one by one in different households. The viewership was still limited. Unlike SITE television which was open for viewing for every villager, these privately owned television sets were only accessible to the television owning households. Firstly limited number of households owned television sets. Entry to these households were only limited to a large extent. Even if the television owner was somewhat liberal, the space available restricted the audience viewing size in the household. When compared to SITE, the telecast time was extended that too in Telugu (regional language). Since, the novelty aspect of television was no longer there, now the audience preference was more towards entertainment, especially films and film songs, dramas and serials. The educational and development programmes on agriculture, animal husbandry, family planning, health and nutrition and education which were telecast before 7:00 PM were watched by fewer number of viewers. Major viewing happened to start taking place between 7 PM to 8:40 PM. The national programme telecast which was largely in Hindi after 8:40 PM was watched by very few viewers. It was because of language difficulty and late telecast unsuitable for the viewers. Unlike SITE, the Doordarshan programmes, with all the attractive advertisement were having a profound effect on viewers' preferences of commodities.

Though significant changes can be seen in the socio-economic life of the village to a large extent, these changes were caused by the impact of Hyderabad city on Kawadapally. The proximity of the village to the city and the growing transport and communication facilities were a major source of change in the village.

9

Summary and Conclusion

India's Satellite Instructional Television Experiment popularly known as SITE is one of the largest experiments on Human communication known so far. As part of the SITE, holistic studies were conducted in selected villages for qualitative evaluation of intended and unintended changes. Fieldwork for the present study was conducted in Kawadapally village of Hayathnagar Block of Hyderabad District (presently Ranga Reddy District) of Andhra Pradesh. Firstfieldwork started in March 1975 and was terminated in October 1976. Second fieldwork was conducted in 1991 for about three months. The process of adoption of development messages, the role played by television in accelerating rural development in areas of agriculture, family planning, health and nutrition and impact of television on school going children and the impact of national programmes on target audiences formed the focus of the study. Television communication which was aimed at affecting behavioural changes was studied. In addition, cultural and development communication processes existing in the village were also studied.

A short re-study was undertaken in Kawadapally. During the re-study an attempt was made to understand the longitudinal changes that had occurred in the village between 1975 and 1991 and to record the continuing effects of television on the village life. Changing methods and process of human communication after 1975 were analysed along with structural and technological changes that had occurred in the village. An overall attempt was to carry out social evaluation and changes that had taken place in the village life. Also efforts were made to understand the role played by television in bringing about these changes. The analysis presented combines data pertaining to the original study and restudy. Some efforts were also made to briefly mention the changes that might have occurred after SITE.

The second study was conducted in Kawadapally fifteen years after the first study. During these fifteen years, the population of Kawadapally increased but the number of households remained almost same. Thereby increase in the household size without increase in total number of households in the village, a social phenomenon characteristic of the Indian village. However, a significant change observed in the village was in the pattern of speech and multilingualism persisting in the village.

Changes were visible in the village economic scene. There was increase in the number of landless household and also there was a decline in those holding larger areas of land. In parallel there was increase in the small, marginal and medium size holdings. There was decline in the number of cultivators and increase in the number of households who depended on labour. Employment showed increase while *Jati* related occupations were on the decline among Scheduled Castes *Jati* and intermediate *Jati.*

In Kawadapally, there was subtle difference in the communication pattern existing between members of larger households where more than one couple would live and the smaller household where generally only one couple and their children lived. In smaller households, the decision-making was shared by husband and wife while it depended on literacy and authority in the kinship structure in the larger household.

Jati level communication was meant for the exchange of information on the availability of boys and girls for the marriage, working arrangements and improvisation of economic conditions. During the restudy period *Jati* communication was more organized in some respects with the entry of *Jati* associations which got themselves affiliated to larger outside bodies. Such *Jati* associations were more welfare oriented and were functioning as an interest group.

At the village level, the communication pattern was between various groups on village level affairs or between leaders and followers. Leaders passed on information to the followers on several topics influencing development. During 1975 study, the Police *Patel*, Mali *Patel* and *Patwari* acted as Information Bridge between government and the village. The *Kawali* (village servant) acted as link between village officials-*cum*-leaders and villagers. By 1991, the hereditary positions of Police *Patel, Patwari* and Mali *Patel* were abolished and a new functionary, the village assistant took over the position of *Kawali* (village servant) that did not continue as a hereditary position. The persons occupying the earlier position still had considerable influence in the village because of their familial importance and they continued to assert their position and often addressed village issues. The drum beaters, washer men and the barber were still utilized for communication by the villagers as well as leaders for various social events like life cycle ceremonies and village festivals.

Mass media like transistors, cinema, and television have been invading the communication scene of the village. The traditional specialists like story-tellers and other folk performers were slowly being replaced by mass media. For example, for festivals like *Sri Rama Navami,* movies were being screened instead of traditional human performances. The traditional communication specialists no longer had social obligation to the village and have commercialized their arts by charging money for their performances.

The information entering into the village finds its way through the individual to the household or group and pervades the village. The time lag depends on the nature of message. The development messages take longer time to get disseminated while messages like death and abnormal behaviour spread quickly. Agriculture fields are the main venues for flow of information among females.

During the 1991 study, information on topics like electricity, power cuts, repairs to the village drinking water pump were of concern for the whole village and were found to be spreading quickly. In several aspects, the communication in the village had become more specialized. Vehicle owners, movie goers, professional persons working in different organizations, pump set owners have their own areas of interest which they discussed amongst themselves.

The village Kawadapally was well exposed to the external world because of its proximity to the city of Hyderabad. This however played a little role in making the development agents of the government active in visiting the village and working for the development of the village. Between 1975 and 1991, the number of employees in the village increased and so also the number of those commuting to Hyderabad daily on various pursuits. More transport facilities were available in the form of buses and private vehicles. The educational services and school enrolments increased. Non-formal education centres, *Aanganwadi* and *Shramik Vidyapeeth* were also spreading literacy and awareness in the village.

Villagers were aware of high yielding varieties of fertilizers and other inputs and some farmers were found purchasing them on their own without any subsidy from development institutions. The presence of irrigation pump sets, tractors and sprayer revealed the progressive side of cultivation. The villagers availed cooperative credit and bank loans for agriculture and animal husbandry. Two abandoned poultry sheds stand witness to the efforts of their enterprising owners. In all these aspects, along with the role played by development personnel, the outside contacts of the villagers, their exposure to television, radio and newspapers cannot be ignored.

There was a threefold increase in the number of radio sets between 1975 and 1991. During 1975, under a project taken up by the National Institute of Nutrition, Hyderabad an Auxiliary Nurse-*cum*-Midwife worked in the village. Villagers used to visit Hyderabad for treatment and pass on information to other villagers about the medical facilities. By 1991, medical services locally available got better with the presence of one MBBS doctor at Abdullapurmet, an RMP doctor and an Ayurvedic practitioner locally. There was growing awareness about nutrition, diseases and their causation. There seemed to be good awareness about family planning despite of the fact that between 1975 and 1991 there was an increase in the number of large households in the village.

Information that television (SITE) would be showing pictures reached the leaders ahead of the villagers. The villagers who were surprised to look at the umbrella shaped mirror (Dish Antenna) became aware of its utility only after pre-SITE telecast started in July 1975. Villagers watched with interest the installation work of technicians. Youth of all *Jati* were quite enthusiastic on inaugural day. Elderly persons reached after listening to the sound and music. There were few elders who kept away even after listening to music. Villagers preferred an employee to operate the television than one of their own villagers. The teachers who were given the responsibility felt it as an unnecessary burden on them. In Kawadapally the location of television in one end of the village in *Harijanwada* resulted in some members of the higher socio-economic strata, especially women staying away. Majority of the viewers were from the age group of 15-35 years irrespective of their literacy. Literates of all age groups viewed television provided their literacy level was below matriculation. Those with higher educational qualification like degree avoided television viewing. Members from household located near television place made it a routine to watch television after eating. Women from higher socio-economic strata and recently arrived daughter-in-laws avoided viewing television along with mothers having small children (aged less than 4 year). All other females irrespective of marital status attended viewing.

In contrast to the single SITE television which facilitated community viewing during 1975-76, the village had 40 television sets by 1991. Contrary to the popular notion that richest households would buy television in Kawadapally, a significant number of television sets were purchased by landless and small farmer households. Those who were involved in trade, various jobs and self-employment appeared prominently among television owners. Fourteen out of forty television owners were illiterate, another eleven studied up to fifth class only. Five studied up to upper primary level and only ten have education of high school and above. Gudati Reddi and Gaondla *Jati* household purchased maximum number of television sets whereas no Scheduled Castes *Jati* household was able to acquire a television. The occupational pursuits of television owning households revealed the growing importance of non-agricultural activities in the village economy, and subsidiary sources of income for cultivators.

During SITE days, television viewing was a village affair. Television enthusiasts used to reach the television place well in advance and gossip while waiting for the television custodian teacher to switch on the television. Because of the novelty factor viewers used to gather in anticipation and used to have discussion for clarification and comments on what they saw on television. Elders remembered with nostalgia the large sized SITE television set visible even from distance.

With the entry of privately owned television sets in the eighties access to television got restricted. The Scheduled Caste *Jati* were adversely affected as they could not watch television later in the houses of other *Jati*. In the case of remaining *Jati* more than *Jati* affiliation, it was the proximity to the television owning household and the equation existing between the households which were important in allowing others to watch television. Availability of space, presence of male members of the household (for females) also restricted the access to neighbours' television. Notwithstanding, these all 84 respondents mentioned that they watched television sometimes or other every day. Fifteen respondents mentioned that they watched television on specific days. Only two respondents said that they were watching morning transmission. School television and UGC programmes had one viewer each.

During SITE period, the viewers preferred the telecast to commence one hour after sunset. 7:30 PM to 9 PM during winter and 8 PM to 9:30 PM during summer were preferred. Rainy season was the worst enemy of SITE viewers. Because of hard seasonal work people were tired and were not inclined to come to television place in the slushy lanes where the possibility of reptiles being present was very high. During 1991 study more than weather it was power failure that affected television viewing, 6.30 PM to 8.30 PM formed the prime viewing time in Kawadapally. Those who were watching television between 5.30 PM to 6.30 PM and 8.30 PM to 9.30 PM were considerably fewer in number. No one claimed that he/she watched television after 9.30 PM.

During SITE period, agriculture, animal husbandry, *burra katha* and folk ballad were preferred programmes. Villagers preferred lecture-*cum*-demonstration programmes rather than discussions and talk shows. During the SITE, it was suggested that emphasis should be given on the method rather than explaining the procedure. A slower pronunciation of words was also liked. Unfamiliar names of pesticides, fertilizers, seeds were repeated several times so that the villagers could remember their names. Timely repetition of agricultural programmes helped adoption of innovations. Such repetitions in special telecasts during morning hours were not liked. Though local dialect was preferred for the regional programmes, language formed no barrier for demonstrations, songs, dances, and ballad and film forms. Mythological stories with music and drama format in any language were welcome to the villagers as they were familiar with the story.

The least liked programmes were *Ghazals* and *Kawwalis* in Urdu, and programmes in Kannada.

In 1991, television viewers in general felt that the Doordarshan programmes were better when compared to SITE programmes. More variety, longer duration were the immediate reasons given. Other reasons include the comfort of sitting inside one's house and colourful advertisements. Films, film songs, news, serials, plays, agricultural and sports programmes were preferred for viewing in that order. Because of transmission of Telegu programmes, Hyderabad programmes were preferred over Delhi Kendra. Among Delhi programmes serials, cricket telecasts, *Mahabharata, Ramayana* and *Tipu Sultan* were remembered. There was not much enthusiasm about the agricultural programmes in Telugu. Those who were free at that time watched them if there was nothing else to do.

During SITE study, it has been observed that though there were multiple messages in single programme, only those which do not involve extra expenditure or inputs were being tried. One handicap for trying was the non-availability of implements shown on television. This point applies to present Doordarshan programmes also. Most of the implements shown in the programmes were either not available in the market or not within the buying capacity of the cultivators. In the absence of personal motivation and encouragement from development departments, cultivators seemed to be least interested in adopting new methods of cultivation. Practices which are simple enough and do not involve much expenditure, had a better chance of acceptance provided the programmes were telecast at appropriate season and time. In such cases, acceptance was possible only if the viewer himself was the decision-maker for the household. Here some of the observations made during SITE social evaluation were significant. Literates generally need persuasion and push from knowledgeable persons. Those with some initial knowledge attempted improved methods irrespective of literacy and age group. Time lag between viewing and practices decreased with literacy. Acceptance of practices was not related to *Jati* but to exposure and literacy. During SITE period, males in 15-24 years age group and literates in 15-44 years age group played a vital role in dissemination of information.

During SITE out of school children were lured to school with other siblings to watch television. Except this, the attendance pattern did not change. The teachers were made aware of the advances in science and the lack of facilities for them to teach these in the local school. The teachers who received training as a part of SITE became aware of scientific knowledge, but they could not follow the instructions in actual practice. They were concerned and discussing more about their allowances. By watching SITE television, the knowledge levels of primary students were found to be enhanced both in curricular and extra-curricular activities. Though the general educational programmes increased the knowledge, it was difficult for children to put ideas they got from television to practice. After seeing the programmes like doll making and hat making children recalled their own skills. The teachers and students during 1991 study were not enthusiastic about the school education programmes. This was because of inconvenient timings and not having access to television. Also the novelty value of television disappeared long back and students preferred film programmes and other sponsored programmes with advertisements.

During SITE, the programmes on national integration had expanded the horizons of villagers whose knowledge about outside world earlier was limited to their *'Rajyam'* (state or province). Due to SITE they were exposed to outside world from different *desam* (countries) speaking different dialects. Villagers became familiar with leaders other than the then Chief Minister of Andhra Pradesh (Mr. J. Vengala Rao) and the then Prime Minister of India (Mrs. Indira Gandhi). But the speeches made by various leaders were resented for their monotony.

Lip synchronization between audio and video was another inconvenience during SITE. In the initial period of SITE, the two audio systems were not fully taken advantage for Telugu language programmes. In the later periods when Kannada dramas were telecast with Telugu commentary they were well received. The films that were telecast on every fourth Sunday were well appreciated though they were Hindi movies. Language became an important factor even in 1991 study. But this was not applicable to Hindi films and film songs. During SITE, it was reported that some of the musical programmes used language in their performances. The SITE telecast increased awareness about health, hygiene and nutrition amongst villagers. But villagers, especially the non-viewers and illiterates expressed indifference. This awareness has not influenced the adoption of the villagers as seen from the increase in the incidence of large families by 1991. With regard to Doordarshan telecasts also villagers' awareness about health, hygiene, nutrition, natal care and immunization was certainly on the increase. Other positive effects of television as seen by the villagers include more sophistication among younger generation in better dresses, cleanliness, activeness, intelligence, better speech ability and pronunciation. Elderly persons opined that because of the equalizing effect of television, children from all *Jati* now appear the same. Certainly television has brought new concepts like fuel conservation, savings, investments and fashion. During 1991, fieldwork period discussions were observed at gossip centres on television news items like Gulf War.

Though majority saw positive changes because of television, a few were able to mention the negative aspects also. Some elders were critical of the youngsters for wasting time on watching television programmes which they could not follow. It is said that because of cricket programmes children were neglecting work and studies. Some also mentioned that girls by watching television were getting familiar with the concept of love marriage and expressed resentment for arranged marriages. Also not liked by the elders were the programmes related to women's rights and activities. It is said that by staying home and watching television women were learning more. Similarly, more awareness among workers, their various demands for better wages and development benefits (especially among Scheduled Castes *Jati)* are being attributed to television. Few elders also opined that after some time elders would not be respected at all by youngsters who are getting influenced by television. Various fashions, hair styles, addresses like 'Mummy' and 'Daddy' were not liked by many. It must be mentioned that because of advertisements youngsters were purchasing many unnecessary items.

SITE has been a novel experience in the village where community viewing facilitated effective discussions and opinion formation on many items which were presented for the first time in the given form (television programme). SITE television is remembered as the poor man's television. The development impetus provided by SITE was significant. But the telecast of Doordarshan programmes within a few years after the completion of SITE, completely overshadowed progressive orientation of the earlier views. The current non-television viewers were able to recollect more SITE programmes than television owners. The present-day Doordarshan programmes, with its ever increasing commercial outlook was a weak successor of SITE especially in instructional areas. On the other hand, in villages like Kawadapally, it was difficult to separately identify the development impact of television, from all pervasive impact of nearby Hyderabad city.

Appendix I

Life Without Television

This section has been taken from M.V.T. Raju's original write up appeared in anthropological methods in communication research (*see* Agrawal, 1985).

SITE telecasts were terminated towards the end of July 1976. The fieldwork for the SITE evaluation continued up to first week of October 1976. During this period, the anthropologist studied the responses of various sections of audience. The villagers got so habituated to the facility for nearly one and half year, that they suddenly felt the absence of television which had become part of their daily routine. The following accounts are about the feelings of different sections of the Kawadapally villagers about the absence of SITE telecasts.

Among the most regular viewers were the members of Madiga *Jati*. With the removal of television set they felt that they lost a light from their area. This is because the *Harijanwada* where they reside was a dark locale at the night fall. The light coming out of the television set used to light a large area of *Harijanwada*. They also missed all the viewers of other *Jati* who rarely came to *Harijanwada* otherwise. Thus, the most affected adult viewers are *Harijans*.

Viewers from other *Jati* expressed the opinion that they lost a source of useful past time during evening time. Youngsters reverted back to their gossip sessions at their residential areas. The elderly members started going to bed early after finishing their dinner. Members of the Gaondla *Jati* who resumed participation in the gossip group expressed that they spent their time during SITE period more meaningfully because of two reasons. Television provided them information and entertainment not available to them earlier. They were able to meet people from other *Jati* at the viewing place without making any special efforts.

The *Harijan* women who got habituated to watch television regularly felt that an entertainment aid has been lost. Television provided them an opportunity to watch movies which they could not have seen otherwise. Residing close to television location, they were able to spend their evening. After television stopped showing programmes they resumed their pre-SITE routine of returning from work, cook food, feed the household members, eat and sleep. In two households, where they faced food shortage, they used to feed the children with available food and were spending their time near television to forget their worries.

Women members of higher *Jati* also felt that they lost a good past-time. Few women used to forget their domestic and social tensions by involving themselves in work during the day time and spending the evenings in front of television. For members of single individual households television provided company and solace. Women in the age group of 25-30 expressed their opinion that they lost a valuable experience. Now, they started their routine of chatting with neighbours after completing their daily chores. This, they did while waiting for their male members to return home after work.

A mention should also be made about an attempt made by some of the viewers who did not like the discontinuation of telecasts, to pressurize the government through politicians, after ascertaining from the anthropologists with regard to the truth about the discontinuation of SITE telecasts. Some members wanted to know whether there was a way to influence the government through politicians so that television would not be removed from the village. They wanted to impress upon the anthropologist their desire to retain television and readiness to make necessary efforts for it.

Children expressed their displeasure about the termination of SITE. They felt bad as they lost something valuable. During SITE they were running towards television place as soon as it was dark. They started spending the time either in playing or going to bed early. For school children, the absence of television especially during summer vacation reminded them of the programmes they viewed. School children liked television as it kept them out of continuous monotonous teaching and also taught them new things. Even the non-school going children like cattle herders missed the new faces and new things.

Even the non-viewers felt the absence of television. Though they were not able to watch television because of personal problems, they were being told about the programmes by children and others. They felt that something which was useful for everyone should not have been removed.

The teachers on one hand were happy that they were relieved of the responsibility, but unhappy for losing a valuable past time. They felt that television had increased and reinforced their knowledge and inspired them too.

A small fraction of the non-viewers, however expressed their happiness over the termination of SITE. These are the parents who were unhappy over late returning of the children to home after viewing television. The children sometimes went without eating their meals and this made the mothers to go and search for them in the audience or wait for them until they returned. These people, it should be noted were not averse to the television, but resented the unhappy experience.

Appendix II

Observations Made from Case Studies during SITE

Agriculture - I: The programme is on transplantation method titled "Hints on Planting Rice" which has repeated six times. First time, itself a post-viewing discussion was taken up. The programmes consisted of five messages. But at adoption stage only three were taken up. One instance of adoption was recorded within two months. After ten months, four households adopted the practice. Since transplantation is the job of females, female viewing behaviour played an important role in adoption. Labourers saw the method and they are willing to gain more knowledge. By this they can stay ahead of others and also will be sought after by landlords. They said they will follow the method only if the land owners ask them to follow. The largest family in the village, which also has largest landholding, is one of the first to adopt this method. In fact, the landlord told the labourers to watch the method so that they can do a better job. The message after some time reached non-viewers also. It can be inferred from the instances that viewers try to accept only those messages which are within their reach and do not involve extra burden.

Agriculture - II: When there are several viewers in the household, one of them at least would try to practice the method shown on television. If outsiders are curious about the practice, it is the head of the household who would claim as motivator. Viewers accept messages that seem to be practical and may recall some of them from their experience and mix-up new method with old ones. During this process one unconsciously distorts the message. Viewers, who watch television more frequently, tend to think about adopting messages provided by television. The information on newly adopted practices would be released only if one seeks it.

Agriculture - III: This case on seed-bed making for tobacco shows how a message attracts the attention of the viewers if it does not require deviating much from the existing practice. Viewers also may try to experiment provided one has the temperament to explore the new method and compare it with old ones. A potential adopter is one who is literate, having physical mobility, media exposure and regular viewer of television. Such persons experiment with new methods without spending much. If there are several messages, the ones with minimum expenditure will be taken up. There is better possibility of adoption if the receiver of the message is younger member with imagination to experiment and is head of the household and decision-maker.

Agriculture - IV: This case is about seed bed making for tomato. It reveals how timely programmes, which are definite improvement over existing method will be adopted. A person who is known as good cultivator and consulted by one and all on cultivation practices himself is the adopter. He could not exactly follow the message as he did not catch the name of the fertilizer from the telecast.

Yogabhyasa - I: Programme on *yogabhyasa* was shown twice every month. Though several tried initially a person with some initial knowledge gained through books adopted the message. In this case, the results obtained increased the credibility. He felt mental peace after practicing *asanas*. The person belongs to lowest socio-economic group but has association with higher *Jati*.

Yogabhyasa - II: Another programme on drinking luke-warm salt water for cleaning stomach was misunderstood by illiterate women. Illiterate men talked about it but did not follow. A literate person adopted the practice.

Nutrition: A case study on cooking method of rice and using green vegetables for better nutrition revealed the cultural beliefs of the people. Message on boiling rice without removing starch water using 'Janatha Pressure Cooker' was received with luke-warm response as it is believed that such rice will cause '*watam*' (a disease of limbs). It is also believed that such rice can be preserved for only a short duration while by removing starch water one can keep rice without spoiling for two days. Green leaves are considered to cause indigestion. The adopters who ignored these cultural beliefs are two younger women from lower socio-economic strata, but have the requisite mobility and personality development. They are from households who were present during 60 per cent of the viewing days.

Appendix III

Village Social Research Household Census 1975, 1991

1	2	3	4	5	6	7

	House Number (if any please write) : What is your name?	
1.2	What is the name of your Muhalla/Pera?	
1.3	Since how long you have been living in the village with your family?	
1.4	Who has responsibility of your household?	
1.5	Does he look after every work of the household?	
1.6	What is the total number of persons who eat and live together in this household? (Write the actual number)	
1.7	Please trace the household genealogy (Age, Education and Name). Kindly circle the household members	

	Sl. No.	*Name*	*Relationship to ego (respondent)*	*Sex*	*Age*	*Education*	*Occupation*
	1						
	2						
	3						
	4						

1.8	What is your religion?	1. Hindu 2. Muslim 3. Sikh 4. Christian 5. Jain 6. Buddhist 7. Specify, if any other
1.9	What is your *Jati* ?	
1.10	What kind of ....are you and what is your *Gotra* or its equivalent? (Before asking add the answer of question 1.9 in blank space, please probe)	
1.11	What are the *Jatis* with whom you have food exchange relationships?	
1.12	What are the *Jati/Jatis* with whom you have marriage relationship?	

(*Contd.*)

Appendix III: *(Contd.)*

1.13	Do you have any first degree relative/relatives (by blood or by marriage) in this village If 'Yes', please give their name and addresses	1. Yes 2.· No Name: ___________ Address: _______________ _______________
1.14	What is your family occupation (Kindly list all the occupations given by the respondents)	
1.15	(If agriculture in question 1.14) Kindly ask about the total land cultivated by the household members.	__________total land
1.16	What was your forefather's occupation?	
1.17	What language do you speak in the house?	
1.18	What language/languages do you speak while in market/business or away from the village?	
1.19	Are there any person/persons in your household who can speak languages other than mentioned in Question 1.17 and 1.18?	
1.20	Observe the house type (*Kachha*, *Pucca*, Mixed asbestos-sheet/tin/hut etc.). Please probe for clarification	
1.21	Is there any radio/transistor in your household? If 'Yes', what kind and how many?	1. Yes 2. No ________total number
1.22	Do you/any member of your household receive any newspaper/weekly etc.? If 'Yes', give details.	1. Yes 2. No ________details
1.23	Does any member of your household go to see movies? If 'Yes', give details.	1. Yes 2. No ________details

Bibliography

Agrawal, Binod C. (ed.) (1985). *Anthropological Methods for Communication Research Experiences and Encounters during SITE*, New Delhi: Concept Publishing Company.

Agrawal, Binod C. and Maleek, M.R. (1986). *Television in Kheda: A Social Evaluation of SITE*, New Delhi: Concept Publishing Company.

Belshaw Cyril, S. (ed.) (1977). The Contribution of Anthropology to Development, In: Mathur H.M. *Anthropology in the Development Process*, New Delhi: Vikas Publishing Company.

Damle, Y.B. (1956-57). "Communication of modern ideas: Knowledge in Indian villages", *Public Opinion Quarterly*, p. 20.

Eislein, E.B. and Topper Martin (1976). "Media anthropology: A symposium", *Human Organization*, Vol. 35: 2, pp. 11-12.

Epstein Scarlett, T. (1973). *South India Yesterday, Today and Tomorrow*, The English Language Book Society and Macmillan (1978), London.

Firth Raymond, E. (1959). *Social Change in Tikapia Restudy of a Polynesian Community After a Generation*, London: Allen & Unwin.

Freeman, D., Margaret Mead and Samoa(1965), *The Making and Unmaking of an Anthropological Myth*, Penguin Books.

Gaikwad, N.R., B.L. Tripathi, Haque, H.M.S. (1973). *Rural Social Structure and Communication in an Indian Village*, Ahmedabad: Indian Institute of Management.

Ghosh, Manmohan (Translated into English) (1951). *The Natyastra: A Treatise on Hindu Dramaturgy and Histrionics Ascribed to Bharata Muni*, Calcutta: Asiatic Society of Bengal.

Gough, Kathaleen (1989). *Rural Change in South East India 1950-1980*, London: Oxford University Press.

Gumprez, John J. (1964). "Religious and social communication in village North India, *The Journal of Asian Studies*, 32:89-97.

Hartman, Paul *et al.* (1988). *The Mass Media and Village Life: An Indian Study*, Leicester: Centre for Mass Communication Research.

Hein, Norvin (1958). "The Ramlila", In *Traditional India: Structure and*

Change, ed. Milton Singer, *Journal of American Folklore,* 71, pp. 279-304 (Special Volume).

Lakshman Rao, Y.V. (1966). *Communication and Development: A Study of Two Indian Villages,* Minneapolis: University of Minnesota Press.

Majumdar, D.N. (1958). *Caste and Communication in an Indian Village.* Bombay: Asia Publishing House.

Marriott, McKim (1959). Changing Channels of Cultural Transmission in Indian Civilization. In Intermediate Socities: Social Mobility and Social Communication, Proceedings of 1959 Annual Spring Meeting of the American Ethnographic Society, pp. 63-73.

Mccormack, William (1959). Forms of communication in Virashaiva Religion, In Traditional India: Structure and change. Milton Singer, Journal of American Folklore, Vol. 71, pp. 119-125 (Special Volume)

Sharma, Suresh Chandra (1987). *Media, Communication and Development.* Jaipur: Rawat Publications.

Sinha, Rewati; Panday, Raman; Kolte, N.V.; Arya, H.P.S. (1976). *Communication in Developmental Administration: A Study of Interpersonal Communication in Three Indian States.* Hyderabad: National Institute of Community Development.

Index